LIGHTS

LIGHTS

Revelations of God's Goodness

Jack Wintz

St. Anthony Messenger Press
Cincinnati, Ohio

Unless otherwise indicated, Scripture citations are taken from the *New Revised Standard Version Bible*, copyright ©1989 by the Division of Christian Education of the National Council of Churches of Christ in the U.S.A., and used by permission.

Scripture texts from *The New American Bible With Revised New Testament*, copyright ©1986 by the Confraternity of Christian Doctrine, are used by permission. Gn 2:7 and Jn 9:6-7 are taken from the *New American Bible*, copyright ©1986, 1970 by the Confraternity of Christian Doctrine, Washington, D.C., and used with permission. Scripture texts from *The New Jerusalem Bible*, published and copyright ©1985 by Darton, Longman & Todd Ltd., and Doubleday, a division of Bantam Doubleday Dell Publishing Group, Inc., are reprinted by permission of the publishers.

"The Canticle of Brother Sun," by St. Francis of Assisi, the quotations from "Praises Before the Office" and the quotations from Celano's *A Second Life of St. Francis* are taken from *St. Francis of Assisi: Writings and Early Biographies*, edited by Marion A. Habig, copyright ©1973 by Franciscan Herald Press, and reprinted with permission of the publisher.

The text of "Morning Has Broken," by Eleanor Farjeon, from *The Children's Bells*, published by Oxford University Press, is used by permission of David Higham Associates, Ltd.

The excerpt from "How Great Thou Art," by Stuart K. Hine, copyright ©1953, 1981, by Manna Music, Inc., is used by permission of Manna Music, Inc.

Quotations from *The Life of St. Francis* and *The Soul's Journey Into God*, by Saint Bonaventure, are taken from *Bonaventure: The Soul's Journey Into God, The Tree of Life, The Life of St. Francis*, translated by Ewert Cousins, copyright ©1978 by the Missionary Society of St. Paul the Apostle in the State of New York, and are used by permission of the publisher of the series, The Classics of Western Spirituality, Paulist Press.

The excerpts from Archbishop Romero's pastoral letter and February 24, 1980, homily, translated by James R. Brockman, are reprinted from *Romero: A Life*, copyright ©1989, with the permission of the publisher, Orbis Books.

Excerpt from "The Secret Sits" by Robert Frost, reprinted from *The Poetry of Robert Frost* edited by Edward Connery Lathem. Copyright ©1970 by Lesley Frost Ballantine. Copyright ©1969 by Henry Holt and Co., Inc. Reprinted by permission of Henry Holt and Co., Inc.

Cover and book design by Mary Alfieri
ISBN 0-86716-269-4

The world is charged with the grandeur of God.
It will flame out, like shining from shook foil....

— Gerard Manley Hopkins,
"God's Grandeur"

Contents

Acknowledgments

M ANY PEOPLE have generously helped and encouraged me during the preparation of this book. To them I owe a large debt of gratitude. Since I dread naming names and ranking people, or leaving important players off the list, my thanks will be general.

Various family members, Franciscan confreres and close friends, as well as coworkers at St. Anthony Messenger Press, have assisted me greatly by reading different versions of the manuscript and offering useful feedback. You know who you are. You have my sincere thanks.

I also want to thank the hundreds of people—relatives, friends, loved ones, companions of the journey—who have been important lights in my life but who are not mentioned by name in this book. Names were necessarily kept to a minimum because of the special nature of the book. It is an autobiography only in the sketchiest sense—in the sense that a few remembered events of my life provided a chronological and narrative thread, however thin, on which to fasten select reflections and musings. Many very significant lights did not make it into the book.

My parents and family members, for example, have all been important lights and blessings in my life. Yet not one was mentioned by name in the main text. So I mention them here: My mom and dad are Paul (died in 1963) and Viola, better known as "Pete and Tillie." My brothers and sisters, oldest to youngest are Paul, Judy, Gary and Tese. (I came second.)

As for the others—my unnamed confreres, mentors, coworkers, relatives and dear friends who have been true lights and companions to me along the way: Forgive me for avoiding the difficult and dangerous task of listing names. You are very much included in my thanks, as the dedication suggests.

Beginnings

I T WAS THE MID 1940's. Bing Crosby was playing a young Catholic priest in *The Bells of St. Mary's*. The Fighting Irish of Notre Dame were a mighty football team. And I was a Catholic school kid and young altar boy at St. Louis Church in little Batesville, Indiana.

I remember being fascinated by the mysterious words that introduce the Prologue of John's Gospel (John 1:1-18): "In the beginning was the Word, and the Word was with God, and the Word was God." At the time, those words started off the "Last Gospel," which was read each day at the end of Mass. Small and simple as my mind was, I sensed something awesome in the words of the evangelist whose sign was the eagle, the sublime bird that soars so high and close to the sun.

Who was this mysterious "Word" through whom "all things came into being" and who was also "life" and "the true light, which enlightens everyone" in this world? My fascination continues today as I still try to understand this "Word" and this "light."

I believe that God's word—indeed, God's light—is

embedded deep within all creation and within ourselves, and our life's mission is to uncover it and let it shine forth. What is a word, after all, but that which expresses the mind and heart of the speaker? In the case of the word of God, it is an expression of God's inmost self, which, I believe, is light and overflowing goodness.

Why *Lights*? The title of this book can suggest all kinds of things, and I hope it does. But *Lights* refers especially to the revelations of God's goodness that have shown forth in the persons, places and events of my own life story. As you meander through these pages, you will encounter a wide mixture of memories and insights. You will see soon enough, however, that everything is tied together by a unifying thread—by the thread of God's light, God's goodness.

Whether I write about nature, other people, an event from my own experience, a passage from Scripture or a story about Saint Francis, my intended focus is always God's light hidden within these realities and seeking to be revealed. It is my conviction that God's word is at the bottom of all our experiences, yearnings and musings— even our struggles and failures—and, if we give the word of God a chance, it will beam forth.

What benefit will you gain from sharing my journey? It was monk-writer Thomas Merton, I believe, who pointed out that when we share what is most personal and private in our story, we are also sharing what is most universal. I trust that the lights encountered on my journey will have relevance for your journey, just as your lights surely have relevance for mine. Do not all of our honest insights and intuitions flow from the same "true light, which enlightens everyone" (John 1:9a)?

At the same time, I lay no claim to having a special grasp of the bottomless mystery of God's word at work in the universe. Even today, after many years of reflecting on this mystery, I can claim no inside track.

A trail of mischief. As a young altar boy in my parish church, I was certainly not up there with the angels and saints. In my own little way, yes, I was attracted to God and tried my best to fathom God's word. But mischief was never far away.

I remember how my fellow servers and I tried to make one another laugh as we sat facing one another across the red carpet of the sanctuary floor, supposedly listening to the sermon. We often made funny faces or faked sneezes or mimicked the mannerisms of the priest. I also remember how a cousin of mine, trying to make me lose my composure, used to bump my Adam's apple deliberately with the Communion plate while I was receiving Communion. Chances are the next day I would pay him back in kind.

Maybe the fact that my boyhood parish and school were run by Franciscan friars and sisters—strong believers in an all-good Creator—might explain how a certain playfulness got smuggled into our relationship with God! Now, as a Franciscan friar myself for over forty years, I can only look back and say: "O God, have mercy on us sinners and mischief-makers—even on my cousin!"

Nor has the mischief stopped. It still trails my life like a shadow. Yet, despite my many shortcomings, I feel inspired to sing the praises of God—and of God's goodness as it shines forth like a string of lights from a world often struggling with darkness.

Our common search for light. Even though I have not hesitated to describe my own Franciscan, Roman Catholic, Christian path toward God, I hope from the start to address a much wider audience. This book is written for men and women of all religious persuasions—for everyone searching for God and seeking glimmers of divine light along the footpath of life.

This kind of search is best pursued in a climate of prayer. For this reason, each chapter ends with a meditation or prayer. The prayers do more than sum up key points of each chapter. They remind us that we are seeking not simply *information* about God, but a deeper *love-relationship* with God. To love God with all our heart is not only the first commandment. It is the finest and most exhilarating part of our journey!

If my prayers are answered, this book will lead you to a greater sense of God's beauty and goodness, a deeper awareness of God's immense love for you and an unexpected lightness in your heart and in your step as you grow closer to the wonderful God who walks with you on your journey and who will love you all the way home!

PRAYER FOR LIGHT

All good and loving God,
may your word speak through these words
and your light shine through these lights.

"Unless the LORD builds the house,
* those who build it labor in vain" (Psalm 127:1).*

Without you, gracious God, there is no light. But
"...with you is the fountain of life;
* in your light we see light" (Psalm 36:9).*

Draw us into your light. Amen.

An Angel of Light

T HE DEATH OF A DEAR FRIEND to cancer in 1991
led to the title of this book. Not Roberta's death,
exactly, but the special light I saw in her inspired the title.
I do not hesitate to call it the light of God within her. I
simply experienced something shining in her so naturally
and beautifully at the time of her death that it impressed
me deeply and even lessened my grief. In fact, my main
memory of Roberta lying in the coffin is the radiant ring of
simple woodland flowers that formed a crown around her
head.

Of course, like so many of her close friends, I shed my
share of tears. But the grief was tempered by almost four
years of slow grieving—from the moment I found out she
had cancer and would lose her right breast. I knew rather
precisely—and with ongoing grief—her journey through
the misery of doctor visits, surgery and chemotherapy, not
to mention her fear, sadness and frustration as the cancer
kept spreading. She spoke of being "brought low" by this
terrible assault on her health and life and physical
integrity. No one loved life more than Roberta or praised

God more for the gifts of health, friends, children, flowers and walks in the woods. And yet she was to die a few months before her fiftieth birthday.

Because of her faith and courage, in both sickness and health, Roberta was a light for me as well as for many, many others. For several years and almost up to the day of her death, she was a compassionate companion of elderly people at a large Cincinnati senior citizens' residence where she was the much-appreciated director.

A week or so before she died, she broke her right arm while turning over on a massage-therapy table—an indication of the toll the cancer was taking on her body structure. It was in the context of this encircling darkness, if you will, that I had the strongest experience of Roberta's light. On the day before she was to die, I left my office at St. Anthony Messenger to visit her in the hospital during my lunch break.

I share with you the following memory of my last visit with Roberta—a memory that I put into writing shortly after her death. Despite the sad context, these recollections remain in my mind as an experience of light and wonder—as something sacred:

> Propped up in the hospital bed with a lunch tray before her, Roberta was, as usual, a gracious hostess to her visitors. Standing beside her bed, I was struck by her lightness and upbeat spirit—this despite her worn body and the fact that the cancer was starting to affect her brain, causing her to mix up names, lose her thread of thought a bit or shut her eyes temporarily out of weariness.

Yet, like a good hostess, she was introducing visitors to each other, keeping the conversation going and being patient with an annoying hospital aide who kept pestering her about filling out her menu for the evening meal.

Meanwhile, she was eating gracefully—now some tapioca, now some fruit salad—even though she was eating left-handed because her right arm was broken. Sometimes a piece of food fell on her hospital gown because her face was numb and her arm unsteady. I would pick the food off her gown and place it on the tray. She was not embarrassed in the least and kept the conversation going smoothly.

My dominant memory of this visit is how light and luminous Roberta was. To me she seemed to be floating—as if already rising high above death's clumsy attempts to draw her into darkness.

A legacy of light. The next day, before I had a chance to visit again, Roberta died. The memory of her lightness has never left me. She was an unusual human being and a true saint, and I believe her loving care still shines on the many people she loved.

The special legacy Roberta left me and many others was the legacy of light. She taught us that despite illness, physical disfigurement and the inevitable process of dying, one can be a luminous, successful and even glorious human. Somehow this makes suffering and death a little less fearsome.

When we think of the risen Jesus, we picture him as full of light, luminous. We know, too, that Jesus' rising was happening even in his suffering and that he was already radiating God's light during the darkness of his dying. And if we go back to the day before Jesus died, we can glimpse God's light in him. We see it in Jesus' last meal with his disciples, in the gracious way he handed over his Body and Blood—totally—to his loved ones through the signs of bread and wine during his last meal. We see it in the washing of his disciples' feet, in his willingness to accept the terrible cup out of love for God and for humankind, and in his words from the cross: "Father, into your hands I commend my spirit" and "Father, forgive them; for they do not know what they are doing" (Luke 23:46b, 34b).

This is the kind of light I witnessed in Roberta's dying. After her death, those who cleared out her apartment gave me a little crystal votive-candle holder that belonged to her. Many months later, on a Sunday morning, I had a candle burning inside the crystal as I was praying in my room at Pleasant Street Friary.

I was searching my mind for a focus for this book, which was then in its earliest conception. Suddenly, I looked down at the candle glowing through the crystal and I thought of Roberta. At the same moment, the word *lights* surfaced in my mind. Immediately, I knew I had a focus and a title for this book—not to mention an angel of light to guide my way.

In Gratitude for Light-Bearers

Loving God,
we thank you for special people in our lives,
people like Roberta,
who bring us light and hope.

Through their generosity and gentle love,
they convey your goodness to us
and so draw us closer to you.

Help us to be
carriers of your light to others. Amen.

Learning to Lighten Up

A BOUT THE SAME TIME that the title *Lights* jumped into my consciousness, I had a silly little dream about an angel. All I can remember of the dream is that a tiny angel—about the size of a hummingbird—was flitting before me, bathed in light. I don't really mean to be disrespectful by calling it a "silly little dream." But there was something amusing and endearing about the little angel. And I remember it with affection.

For many years now, I have taken dreams seriously. I believe they come from deep within us, from our deepest self, from the part of our being where the word of God manifests itself within us. They are messages from our deepest inner voice which, my intuition tells me, is part of God's voice and light within us.

Wise people have been telling us for years—indeed for centuries—that God's light can shine through our dreams if we take the effort to uncover their meaning. In the Book of Genesis, the patriarchs Jacob and Joseph discover this.

For several months, I wrestled with my angel dream, praying and reflecting on it, trying to tease out its meaning, never doubting for a moment that God was trying to enlighten me through it. For over a year, I tried to work it into a poetic format. Poetry seemed to me a good way to get at its meaning, especially since my life at that moment seemed to be passing through a gloomy and prosaic valley.

As a former English teacher, I know that these lines, as well as other poetic passages in this book, will never end up in a collection of the world's great poetry. Yet, I use this form of expression because it seems the best way to convey an experience that has enlightened me and set me free. Maybe it can do the same for you.

Carrier of God's Light

An angel appeared to me in a dream
Fresh from God and tiny as a hummingbird.
It flitted vibrantly before me for a moment—
A brilliance shining against my gloom—
And was gone.

Why, little angel, did you enter my dreams?
Why did you come to me?
Was it to correct my grown-up theology
That has been gently nudging angels
Back into the Dark Ages?

You come to remind me of a deeper belief:
That my God is a God of overflowing goodness—
A God of mystery and surprises!
And, Dream Angel, are you not also
Trying to tell me to "lighten up"—
To open up to God's messengers of light?

For what are angels but God's announcers
And carriers of light to a world
Bristling with God
But often not seeing God
Because eyes have grown dim, closed and
　　unexpectant.

As Christmas rolls around,
Some weeks after my dream,
I find my eyes growing bigger and brighter
And my soul growing lighter.
For as I read the Gospel accounts
Surrounding Christ's birth, I suddenly notice
That they are filled with myriads of angels—
Angels appearing to Joseph and Mary and Zechariah,
Angels appearing to the Magi,
Angels appearing, especially, to simple shepherds—
Angels that seemed to have flown in straight from
　　God's throne,
Still shimmering and dripping with divine light!

I begin to catch the bright message
Of my Dream Angel in subtle little ways:
In the gleam of stars, the smile of a child,
In the jingle of tiny bells,
In a friend's handclasp or embrace.
Most of all, God's message and my Dream Angel
Converge on Christmas day during worship
In the magical voice of a black singer,
A soloist in a mixed Gospel choir.
He sings "O Holy Night"
With a voice that lilts with brightness and power.
My heart soars along with his voice
To a most delicious height where—finally—
His voice rings out with my dream's message:

"O hear the angels' voices!"

Yes, that is it, very simply:
I was told to hear the angels' voices,
To open my heart to God's light and goodness,
In all its manifestations,
Minute by minute, in the mist of my days.

So I'm trying to stay in touch
With my little hummingbird angel:
To lighten up,
To savor God's beauty wherever it appears,
To smell the roses along the way!

Angels are "in." I find it curious that my dream occurred at a time of growing interest in angels. At the very moment I was exploring the meaning of my dream, *Time* magazine ran a cover story on "The New Age of Angels." And *Newsweek* also ran a major story on angels on the exact same publishing date! What's going on here?

In discussing angels, it seems to me, the best place to focus attention is not on the angels themselves—their shape, size or manner of existence—but on what they tell us about God: that God never lets us sit alone in the dark. God is always there caring for and loving us— communicating to us light and healing energy.

Throughout the Scriptures God's significant acts of saving love are announced to humankind by "an angel of the Lord." No matter how awesome the gap between heaven and earth, there are always angelic bridges carrying the message to us, translating God's plan in ways that we can understand. They carry to us, as they carried to the shepherds, the Good News that a Savior-God is with us. It is the same kind of message Zechariah relayed to the world when he announced that:

the dawn from on high will break upon us
to give light to those who sit in darkness and in the
shadow of death (Luke 1:78b-79).

PRAYER OF THANKS FOR ANGELS

We thank you, God,
for the many angels of light you send us.

We thank you for being yourself
our foremost source of light—
a protector who never sleeps.

We praise you, as well,
for sending your own Son to walk with us
as our guiding light.

We embrace you
and all your gifts of light. Amen.

Woods

F ROM MY EARLIEST YOUTH, I have always been
fascinated by the woods. They reveal to me, more than
any other part of nature, the mystery and beauty of God.
The woods, I believe, have a special place in the mind of
God. The earliest story in the Bible takes place in a
woodland of sorts, the Garden of Eden.

When I step into a forest, it's like stepping into the
mystery of the Creator's mind. It's like traveling into the
word of God, into that awesome primordial blueprint from
which all things were made.

I have wonderful memories as a youngster, twelve or
fourteen years old, walking into the woods of southern
Indiana with my dad—ever so quietly—at the crack of
dawn. The purpose was to hunt, but I was always taken up
most by the mysterious wonder of this sacred setting.

The air was crisp, and mist hung amid the dark timbers
like clouds of incense as the first shafts of sunlight peered
through the forest ceiling. Dew covered the green branches
of the underbrush and I felt its cold wetness as we crept
along in hushed silence. Birds and squirrels and other

creatures began stirring around us. In the distance, we could hear the cawing of crows or a farmer opening a barn door or a car rumbling over a covered bridge.

My young mind was always filled with awe in this setting. Being shy, fearful and introverted, I found going into the woods something of a passing into my own mysterious inner life and into the feelings awakened by the natural world. It was a private, comfortable, secret, safe place to be—away from the intrusive proddings of grownups.

Nature springs from the word. In their own way, though I was hardly conscious of it, the woods were linking me with the Source of life, with that primordial moment when all creatures emerged from the word. The song "Morning Has Broken" says it with simple power:

> Morning has broken
> Like the first morning,
> Blackbird has spoken
> Like the first bird.
> Praise for the singing!
> Praise for the morning!
> Praise for them, springing
> Fresh from the Word!

We sense the crack-of-dawn mystery that these words convey. We can almost see "springing fresh from the word" the whole of God's creation: the mist and the trees, the lakes and the mountains, the deer and the swans. These are like sacred ideas that nature and God's word have insisted on for centuries—to blend Henry David Thoreau with Saint John.

Books of my soul. I don't know who originated the concept or the quotation, but I have often been attracted by the formula: "Scripture and nature: two books of my soul." This truth has always found a deep echo in my heart. No doubt those of us who are Christian feel at home with the notion that our Scriptures are the book of God's word, with the life and teachings of Jesus, the Incarnate Word, the summit of God's biblical revelation.

We are a bit less familiar with the idea that God's word is also revealed in the book of nature. Yet saints and poets and Scripture writers have been communicating this message all along. Saint Paul, for example, wrote to the Romans: "Ever since the creation of the world his eternal power and divine nature, invisible though they are, have been understood and seen through the things he has made" (1:20).

Saint Francis praised God through "Brother Sun" and described this great light in the sky as an amazing sign of the Most High himself. He saw God's wisdom, moreover, expressed in all brother and sister creatures. Indeed, Francis saw in the beauty of a flower the One who is Beauty itself. Saint Bonaventure, according to Franciscan theologian Zachary Hayes, considered the cosmos the "primal book of divine self-revelation."

Much earlier, the Book of Wisdom labelled "naturally stupid" all those who "from good things seen, have not been able to discover Him-who-is, or, by studying the works, have not recognized the Artificer" (13:1b-c, *New Jerusalem Bible*).

When I was a youngster wandering, often alone, through the woods and along the streams of Indiana, I was not conscious of the mystery of God playing on my soul. But on some level, I sensed that the Creator was no farther away than the nearest leaf swaying in the breeze or the mosquito lighting on my neck. I was particularly awestruck whenever a summer rainstorm overtook me in the woods. A heavy rain plunging through the forest would take me back into a world of primordial mystery and Eden-like innocence that could not have been far from the word of God. Later, I put those feelings into a poem:

Rain in the Forest

From aching toil in town I fled—
Deep into the woods where the rain
Crashed through the hickory grove
And fell on gleaming ferns and underbrush.

I inhaled the wet scent of drenched slabs of stone
And of the soaked forest floor
And pine needles on the ridge.

Dry under protective branches, I listened to the rain
Roaring through the trees
And watched it soak into mossy banks.
I saw through black timbers,
How it fell in sheets through the clearing
Against waving ghosts of green.

Through the rain I admired the blackberry stalks

At the edge of the clearing
And gazed at their fresh wet leaves
And the wild berries, dripping and glistening.

A lash of thunder cracked through the rain,
And the rain roared down at a fiercer pace,
Sending misty shivers up my spine.
I became one with the dripping leaves
And the cleansing, healing rain—
And the Mystery from which they came,
Forgetting for a moment that Adam had fallen
And I could not stay here forever.

PRAYER OF PRAISE FOR GOD'S CREATION

Loving Creator,
I see your beautiful Word hidden in the depths of
*   nature,*
and ever budding forth.

With the old melody echoing within me,
I lift my heart in song:

When thro' the woods and forest glades I wander,
And hear the birds sing sweetly in the trees;
When I look down from lofty mountain grandeur
And hear the brook and feel the gentle breeze;
Then sings my soul, my savior God, to Thee;
"How great Thou art! How great Thou art!" Amen.*

Brian

FATHER BRIAN IRVING, O.F.M., was my science and physics teacher at the high school seminary in Cincinnati during the early 1950's. I present him as one of the special lights I encountered along life's path. This Franciscan friar stands out as an example of how the word of God can shine forth in special humans and, through them, guide other travelers on their way.

I had entered the seminary at fourteen to give the Franciscan priesthood a try. I had left my family and boyhood chums back in Batesville, some fifty miles away. During my junior year at St. Francis Seminary I somehow strayed into a dark valley of negativity and discouragement. I was on the verge of giving up the idea of being a priest. During my three-month summer breaks, I always got strongly reconnected with my family, relatives and boyhood chums at Batesville. I was in love with sports of all kinds and played baseball for my hometown's Junior American Legion team. One summer we nearly made it to the state finals. I was even more interested in basketball, known in Indiana as "Hoosier hysteria."

A strong longing came over me to hang out and play basketball and other sports at the local high school with my old buddies in Indiana rather than continue at the seminary.

I began finding more and more things to be negative about. I grew more surly by the day, choosing to tap into the darkness rather than the light, sinking into an ugly cynicism about everything from the food in our refectory to our seminary basketball uniforms. Finally I reached the point of deciding to quit the seminary. I wrote my parents and informed them that I wanted to come home.

Brian enters the scene. My parents—concerned about what was best for me—shrewdly went into a stalling pattern. They also urged me to seek counsel before making a hasty decision in a moment of darkness. My fellow seminarians, who were often going through similar crises, singled out Brian as the person who would be caring and understanding.

Brian was popular with the students because he was always willing to roll up his sleeves and give himself over to student activities, whether it was tennis or softball or working on a car. His hair was prematurely speckled with gray. His caring eyes, ever watching behind rimless glasses, did not miss much. And he always had a sly little smile and tilt of the jaw which seemed to say: "I'm two steps ahead of you, brother!"

I don't remember much about the conversations that took place between Brian and me. I just recall that he was respectful and humble, and dealt with me like an equal and someone he cared about. Nor do I recall how many days or weeks my personal crisis lasted, but Brian had time to observe my negativity and how I was turning sour on almost everything. One evening when I stopped by to say hello to him in the physics lab where he was setting up experiments for the next day's class, he took me aside and simply said: "You're not giving God a chance."

Those are the only words I remember from our discussions. But how those words scattered my darkness! They did not seem preachy or scolding but simply full of gentle truth and light. I felt instinctively that Brian's soul was for my soul. As I look back now, some forty years later, I see Brian in my imagination and heart dissolving into a glowing image of the Good Shepherd, ready to lay down his life for the sheep.

From that moment I began turning from the darkness and negativity that I was nursing so zealously in myself, and began trying to follow the lead of God's light within me, my surroundings and in the rest of my Ohio friends. Maybe I still wasn't sure that my ultimate goal was the priesthood or Franciscan life, but I knew it would be a mistake to leave on the basis of self-nurtured negativity.

Later encounters with Brian. Interestingly, after my ordination as a priest some eleven years later, my path from time to time crossed Brian's in significant ways.

As a young priest just starting to try out my wings, I took some summer courses in journalism at Marquette University in Milwaukee. During that same summer, Brian was across town taking advanced physics courses. He went out of his way, as was his nature, to initiate get-togethers with me. He suggested that we meet at a simple little place (I believe it was called the Tuxedo Bar) where we shared deep-souled camaraderie over the city's nationally known beers. His fraternal care, once again, offered a gentle lift to my heart at this important juncture of my just-begun Franciscan ministry.

Two years later, we taught in the same high school together, but not for too long. Brian soon felt called to volunteer for missionary work in the Philippine Islands. As I see it now, this was just one more expression of his generous self-giving nature.

About two years later, because of an unrelated opportunity, I too found myself in the Philippines for a three-year stint as a teacher in a Franciscan seminary. Though we were working on different islands, Brian and I were able to share significant moments together.

This included his final, rather sudden, encounter with cancer. He entered a Manila hospital to undergo exploratory surgery, or so he thought. When he woke up from the operation, he discovered that more than half his stomach had been removed because of cancer and, even worse, a serious infection had set in.

Brian's final days. Though dealing with the sudden information that he probably only had days, maybe hours, to live, he nevertheless offered love and attention to the few visitors who came. He welcomed me as fraternally as ever when I entered the room, still wearing his sly smile and showing no signs of self-pity. He and another friar who had come with him from the island of Leyte were engaged in a dialogue that was surprisingly energetic and good-natured, given the circumstances.

Brian died the next day. A few days later, in a great show of fraternity, a large number of Franciscan friars from various countries who were ministering in the Philippines gathered for the funeral and buried Brian with reverence and affection in a Manila cemetery.

What is the meaning of Brian's journey? How assess this man, born in Wichita, Kansas, who spent a life of self-giving, died and was buried in a far-off land? To me, his life-pattern mirrored that of the eternal Word. For that Word, in a way of speaking, left the divine homeland behind to join the human enterprise on earth as the Word made flesh. The Word made flesh then poured out his life for the sake of others, died and was buried in his adopted land. To die in land not your own, far from home—is this not a symbol of selling all one has (as Jesus recommended to the rich man in the Gospel) and handing oneself over to the service of others?

The Word of God, the Light of the world, is like the self-communicating sun, spending itself generously to bring glorious light and warmth and life to the world. Brian was like the sun.

God of love and dearest of friends,
we thank you for your providential love.

We thank you for giving us caring friends
and counselors who guide us
at difficult points of our journey.
They bring love and sunshine into our days.

Show us, as well,
how to be good friends to others.

Draw us into deeper friendship with you. Amen.

'Let There Be Light'

T HE SCRIPTURES SAY A LOT about *light* and *word*,
two central themes of this book. I invite you to
meditate with me upon these two ideas.

In the Book of Genesis light is the first thing God
creates. Interestingly, this "first creation," as well as all
those that follow, is accomplished by the word: God
simply *says*: "Let there be light" (see Genesis 1:3). We are
reminded of the formula announced in John's Gospel: that
all things were created through the Word (see John 1:3).

What is Genesis trying to tell us here? Is the creating of
light first a poetic way of saying that light is something
primary in the identity of God? We refer to God, after all,
as Eternal Light.

Looking at creation itself, are the Scriptures hinting to
us that light is the primary core of all created being? Is
there any link between this gift of created light and the
vibrating energy physicists affirm to be at the heart of all
created matter, including our own? And is not this
pulsating light revealing itself today in millions of glowing
TV and computer screens that instantly unite people to

each other through an internet of energy?

Even setting these musings aside, we can't deny the fact that in Genesis light leads off the long list of God's creation. If all creation somehow flows from light, it would seem wise of us to turn greater attention to the primacy of light in our universe—to take note of the "light cues" that we encounter day by day on our journey.

Do not our very souls brighten in response to light? And this seems to be the case whether the light be that coming from sun, sky and stars or from the wise words and comforting smiles of friends.

Do not our lives grow brighter as we tap the light we see about us rather than the darkness? Our own inner light seems to flame higher as we learn to appreciate and give praise for sunny days, for flowers dancing in the sunlight, for glowing rivers and lakes—for humor, too, which lightens the heart and disarms sad souls feeding on negativity.

Our hearts vibrate with joy as we go out to meet the sunrise or as we light a candle or throw open closed shutters. Our souls grow brighter as we notice how the sunlight plays—or the rain glistens—on the leaves of trees. We become more joyful and alive as we let this light soak into our beings!

We are wise to move toward those people, places and things that radiate God's light and beauty and let them guide us as we make choices about our life's direction. If something beautiful attracts our souls and we ignore it, are we not voting for the darkness? Are we not sinning against the light? We do our spiritual health a favor when we follow our heart's desire to visit our favorite overlook or flower garden or take that stroll along the beach.

The Incarnate Word and light. Just as the light shining from the book of nature cheers our hearts, so all the more should the light known as the incarnate Word, Jesus Christ, do the same. Both of these lights are one, revealing, as they do, the one word of God.

Jesus openly says to the people: "I am the light of the world. Whoever follows me will never walk in darkness but will have the light of life" (John 8:12). Jesus proclaims that he is the exact word—or mirror—of God, saying to Philip, "Whoever has seen me has seen the Father" (14:9b). This is the very point John makes as he concludes his Prologue: "No one has ever seen God. It is God the only Son, who is close to the Father's heart, who has made him known" (1:18).

Christ's light, Christ's values are so familiar to us and so pervasive that we often take for granted the amazing guidance that they offer us. If you or I were in a thick forest when darkness suddenly fell, we would quickly realize the blessing of light. For we would be bumping into trees, straying into spider webs, tripping over logs or falling off creek banks. With the return of light, however, finding our way is nearly effortless!

In the same way, if the light of Christ were suddenly taken away, we would be groping and stumbling in a dark world. Vengeance and hatred and social chaos would replace peace and love and order. Fortunately, we have the light of Christ in the Gospels and in the community of the faithful. And therefore we are able to see clearly the wise and loving paths we should follow.

In John's Gospel, which is filled with symbols of light and darkness, Jesus is often presented as the Light of the World, as one bringing sight to the blind. Judas Iscariot, on the other hand, rejects the light and chooses darkness. Indeed, when Judas flees the warm fraternity of Christ at the Last Supper, John simply writes: "And it was night" (John 13:30b). At the end of Jesus' public life, John has Jesus sum up his mission with this simple image: "I have come as light into the world, so that everyone who believes in me should not remain in the darkness" (12:46).

PRAYER FOR OPENNESS TO THE LIGHT

Loving God,
we are surrounded by your light,
which is also deep within us.

Like flowers we bask in your light.

Send your radiance into our souls
that we may become more luminous, bright for others.

At one with you, we proclaim:
"Let there be light!" Amen.

God's Word Gets Results

I N GENESIS, as in other books of Scripture, there is no "hang time" between God's word and its accomplishment. God says, "Let there be light," and there is light! When God speaks, creation leaps into existence. God's word is active and effective. It achieves its goals.

Isaiah put this idea forward dramatically in a celebrated passage of the Hebrew Scriptures that foreshadows the heaven-to-earth movement of the Word becoming flesh. God's mouthpiece, Isaiah, says:

> For as the rain and the snow come down from
> heaven
> and do not return from there until they have
> watered the earth,
> making it bring forth and sprout,
> giving seed to the sower and bread to the eater,
> so shall my word be that goes out from my mouth;
> it shall not return to me empty,
> but it shall accomplish that which I purpose,
> and succeed in the thing for which I sent it.
> (Isaiah 55:10-11)

Franciscan Spiritual Center
6902 SE Lake Road Suite
Milwaukie, OR 97267-214

In Jesus, we certainly see God's Word come down to earth and move actively toward its ultimate and triumphant goal. Jesus himself is the perfect example of God's Word—or plan—being realized on earth.

As we watch Jesus carrying out his public ministry and mission, we have indeed a powerful picture of the unstoppable progress of God's word. Totally responsive to God's will, Jesus moves relentlessly toward Jerusalem to fulfill God's plan till he exclaims at last from the cross, "It is finished" (John 19:30b).

Parables of the word. Jesus describes this resolute unfolding of God's plan in his parables about the reign of God. Jesus likes to use the image of seeds—tiny grains that contain within themselves a built-in dynamism for achieving their goal. Jesus tells us later that these seeds represent God's word and the growth of God's Kingdom.

Take the following parable, for example. The seed seems to be programmed to produce the desired results! Jesus says, "The kingdom of God is as if someone would scatter seed on the ground, and would sleep and rise night and day, and the seed would sprout and grow, he does not know how. The earth produces of itself, first the stalk, then the head, then the full grain in the head. But when the grain is ripe, at once he goes in with his sickle, because the harvest has come" (Mark 4:26-29).

Even when we are not conscious of it, the parable indicates, God's word, God's plan is moving forward by some inexorable energy of its own. God's word, therefore, is not so much an idea being expressed as a plan marching into action.

And so the word of God in Scripture is not to be read simply as information but also as an invitation to action. The word sweeps us into the divine action—if we let it. Consider Jesus' parable about the sower going out to sow. Jesus again seems to pick up on the word-and-seed metaphor of Isaiah. He describes as "the word of God" the seed falling on the path, among thorns, on shallow ground—and on rich ground.

Nothing is more tragic, the parable suggests, than for God's seed to be scattered about and all that dynamism to go to waste! Why? Because no one responds or gets engaged. On the contrary, how wonderful and triumphant the seed falling on rich soil—on those who "hold it fast in an honest and good heart, and bear fruit with patient endurance" (see Luke 8:15).

PRAYER FOR RICH SOIL

Praise to you, Creator God,
for the dynamic seed of your word
planted deep within our world and within me.

Help me provide rich soil for this seed
so it can be efficacious.

I embrace your plan within me.

To paraphrase Saint Paul (Philippians 1:6),
I am confident that the loving God
who began a good work in me
will bring it to completion
by the day of Jesus Christ. Amen.

The Light of Saint Francis

O N A HOT AUGUST AFTERNOON in 1954, a brown Franciscan habit was placed over me in an investiture ceremony at St. Anthony Novitiate in Cincinnati. I was eighteen years old. Invested with me were eleven classmates with whom I had graduated from St. Francis Seminary High School two months earlier. We would be spending one entire year in the novitiate, learning about prayer and Franciscan spirituality.

Our venerable brick novitiate building, built in the late nineteenth century, stood atop a hill overlooking Mt. Airy Forest—a vast city woods that spreads out for miles over rolling hillsides. A love for beautiful natural settings is part of the Franciscan tradition.

The brown habit and white cord which I received that day in 1954 have always been an important symbol for me. Though falling forever short of the ideals it represents, I have for more than forty years been entranced by the Franciscan legacy woven into the fibers of the habit. Above all, I have admired the spirit of Saint Francis of Assisi, who founded the Franciscan Order in the thirteenth century.

Next to Jesus Christ, Francis has been for me the greatest conveyer of God's light and goodness. Francis mirrored so brilliantly and joyfully the light of Christ!

The man behind the birdbath. Saint Francis has been a special light not only for me but also for millions of other people all around the world—people of almost every religious persuasion. Matthew Arnold, the nineteenth-century British poet, called Francis "a figure of most magical power and charm" with an amazing ability to "fit religion for popular use."

Perhaps the most popular sculptured image of Francis is that of the ragged little man standing on a birdbath. This figure, which has become so universal, could be discovered as easily in a Methodist's backyard or a Buddhist prayer garden as at a Franciscan retreat center.

To those who grumble that this birdbath art is too low-brow and sentimental, I say, "Lighten up! Francis belongs to the popular arts as much as with the fine arts—and he certainly belongs to the birds." To set Francis on a birdbath or in a flower garden or to depict him with birds circling around his head is just a popular way of saying: "This man had a special link with all of God's creatures, and it's just like him to be standing there among them."

Francis was in awe of the swallow and cricket and rabbit. "Where the modern cynic sees something 'buglike' in everything that exists," observed the German writer-philosopher Max Scheler, "St. Francis saw even in a bug the sacredness of life."

Another reason Francis should keep his place on the birdbath or amid the daffodils is that his being there helps us see, as Francis himself did, that the world of nature and the world of God are one. Francis did not fall into the trap of dualism, which creates an artificial wall between the natural world and the supernatural, the secular and the sacred. For Francis, every creature was sacred. The world he lived in was not something wicked to be rejected but a sacred ladder leading to its Creator.

Francis would say that the birds coming to the birdbath are holy. Water is holy. Bugs are holy. Why shouldn't Francis be there in the garden where he can be pelted by the rain or sleet or kissed by the sun and wind or a passing butterfly?

In 1992 the Catholic Bishops of the United States published a statement on the environment entitled *Renewing the Earth*. In it, they praised Saint Francis and emphasized: "Safeguarding creation requires us to live responsibly in it, rather than managing creation as though we are outside it." We should see ourselves, they added, as stewards within creation, not as separate from it. Francis was ahead of his time. He saw himself, as do today's ecologists, as a part of the ecosystem, not as some proud master over and above it.

Francis addressed creatures as "brother" and "sister"— as equals, not subjects to be dominated. And that's why the humble figure of Francis standing at the birdbath or among the plants and shrubs is so right for our day. He truly saw himself as a simple servant and steward of creation—little brother to the birds and the fish and the lowly ivy. Saint Francis reminds us that we are a part of our environment and are called to love and protect it.

Patron saint of ecology. In 1979 Pope John Paul II proclaimed Francis of Assisi the patron of ecology. The pope cited him for being "an example of genuine and deep respect for the integrity of creation.... Saint Francis," he added, "invited all creation—animals, plants, natural forces, even Brother Sun and Sister Moon—to give honor and praise to the Lord."

Francis did precisely this in grand style, in his famous *Canticle of Brother Sun* addressed to all the creatures:

> Most high, all-powerful, all good, Lord!
>> All praise is yours, all glory, all honour
>> And all blessing.
>
> To you alone, Most High, do they belong.
>> No mortal lips are worthy
>> To pronounce your name.
>
> All praise be yours, my Lord, through all that you
> have made,
>> And first my lord Brother Sun,
>> Who brings the day; and light you give to us
>> through him.
> How beautiful is he, how radiant in all his splendour!
>> Of you, Most High, he bears the likeness.
>
> All praise be yours, my Lord, through Sister Moon
> and Stars;
>> In the heavens you have made them, bright
>> And precious and fair.

All praise be yours, my Lord, through Brother Wind
    and Air,
        And fair and stormy, all the weather's moods,
        By which you cherish all that you have made.

All praise be yours, my Lord, through Brother Fire,
        Through whom you brighten up the night.
        How beautiful he is, how gay! Full of power and
            strength.

All praise be yours, my Lord, through Sister Earth,
    our mother,
        Who feeds us in her sovereignty and produces
        Various fruits and colored flowers and herbs.

All praise be yours, my Lord, through those who
    grant pardon
        For love of you; through those who endure
        Sickness and trial.
Happy those who endure in peace,
        By you, Most High, they will be crowned.

All praise be yours, my Lord, through Sister Death,
        From whose embrace no mortal can escape.
Woe to those who die in mortal sin!
        Happy those She finds doing your will!
        The second death can do no harm to them.

Praise and bless my Lord, and give him thanks,
        And serve him with great humility.

PRAYER OF SOLIDARITY WITH CREATURES

We thank you, loving God,
for giving us the family of creation
as our sisters and brothers,
for surrounding us with birds and trees
and flowers and mother earth.

We thank you for teaching us through Saint Francis
that our praise and thanks sound sweetest to you,
when we pray not in proud isolation,
but as part of the symphony of creation. Amen.

The Secret of Saint Francis

I N AUGUST 1955, when my year of novitiate was completed, I drove with my mom and dad and family members to Duns Scotus College in Detroit. The school was named after John Duns Scotus, a leading Franciscan philosopher and theologian of medieval Europe. Duns Scotus College was the school of philosophy for the Cincinnati-based Franciscan Friars of St. John the Baptist Province, to which I belonged.

Beginning my four-year stay at Duns Scotus was like entering medieval Catholic Europe. This was borne out by everything from the school's patron, to its Latin philosophy books, Gregorian chants, monastic life-style and lovely medieval architecture. Brown-robed instructors with names like Effler, Ramstetter and Blumlein were reminders to us friar students that our province of Franciscans sprang during the 1800's from German-speaking lands.

The hidden wellspring of Francis' spirit. A key memory of my years at Duns Scotus was the visit of an old white-haired Franciscan friar from Germany who one evening was invited to speak to the student body about the spirit of Saint Francis. The major point that he shared with us, in his broken English, was his belief that the overflowing goodness of God was the real secret behind the saint's spirituality.

Those words—"the overflowing goodness of God"—which the friar repeated often, were a special source of illumination for me. And from that moment on, without fail, my intuition has kept telling me: "Yes, this is it—as far as I'm concerned, this is the secret of Saint Francis!" After years of testing this intuition on experiences of Franciscanism in various countries and cultures, I keep coming back to the same conviction.

For me, Francis' burning sense of God's overflowing goodness is the wellspring of his spirituality and the clue to almost everything about the saint: his joy in poverty, his reverence for nature, his love for the poor, his generosity, his optimism, his poetry and exuberance, his affectionate style of prayer, his burning love of the crucified Jesus.

The idea of God's overflowing goodness is not particularly new. It lies at the heart of the Christian revelation. What is original with Saint Francis, perhaps, is the intensity and emotion with which he experienced that revelation.

God's outpouring of goodness from the cross. Shortly after Francis' conversion, that is, after he left behind his wild and worldly life and dedicated himself totally to God and to the service of poor lepers, he was praying with great emotion in a solitary wooded spot. He had a vision in which Christ began looking at him from the crucifix with such love that Francis' "soul melted," as his biographer Saint Bonaventure tells us.

From then on, Francis would often fall into tears as if that experience of God's incredible love and goodness were forever branded on his soul. The God Francis experienced was the God who chose to be poor—who poured out everything out of love for humankind and held back absolutely nothing. This caused the little saint to go about weeping and proclaiming that "Love is not loved"— that God is madly in love with human beings and we don't respond. This lavish, unconditional love is the major revelation that Francis saw shining forth from the Word made flesh and indeed through all of creation.

Francis' infatuation with God's goodness is reflected time and again in his exuberant prayers. In one prayer, he suddenly starts repeating, if not babbling, the word *good*, as if intoxicated by it. He prays:

> All powerful, all holy, most high and supreme God, sovereign good, all good, every good, you who alone are good, it is to you we must give all praise, all glory, all thanks, all honor, all blessing; to you we must refer all good always. Amen.
>
> ("The Praises Before the Office")

The atheist looks behind the face of reality and sees a black void. The agnostic looks and sees a big question mark. Most of us who consider ourselves believers in God try to see something good and hopeful behind the mask of

45

reality, but our vision is often dimmed by doubt. Francis of Assisi looks behind the mask and sees amazing grace—the overflowing goodness of God. That is why this poet-saint goes about creation filled with joy, like a minstrel singing God's praises.

I've tried to capture Francis' faith-vision in the following lines:

What Francis Saw Behind the Veil of Creation

When Francis looked behind the veil of the blue sky
and the glowing sun, he saw God's unconditional love.
If Francis, in his mind's eye, were to scratch
through the surface of an apple, a rose
or a butterfly's wing,
he would fall to his knees and cry out:
"Holy, holy, holy,"
for he would see there the blinding beauty
of God's overflowing goodness.
Above all, when Francis gazed behind the figure
of his crucified God—behind the blood and thorns—
he would only weep and weep and weep!
For there he saw the roaring furnace of God's love.

PRAYER TO KNOW GOD'S GOODNESS

All good and gracious God,
give us the vision of Saint Francis
that we might better see your goodness and benevolence
at the heart of reality.

Trusting in your all-out love for us,
may we fall more deeply in love with you
and serve you with greater joy and praise. Amen.

Finding God's Goodness in Me

A T THE END of our novitiate year, my classmates and I had taken temporary (three-year) vows of poverty, chastity and obedience. During our time of temporary vows, which would be completed after our third year at Duns Scotus College, the larger decision as to whether or not we should take final vows hung over our heads like clouds that changed hues according to the weather in our souls.

It was a period of great self-questioning for each of us, especially each time a classmate decided to discontinue the Franciscan life, leave the seminary and pursue happiness in that big world out there "beyond the walls." Several times I was deeply shaken by the departure from the order of some of my dearest classmates. Yet, through the mystery of God's providence, I continued to be attracted to the gospel life as a Franciscan friar.

Struggling with natural urges. At the same time, however, another turbulence was boiling up inside of me. The spiritual writers of those days would have called it temptations of the flesh. I was keenly aware of natural drives and urges and fantasies within me that caused many a sleepless night and made me fret about the state of my soul and whether I was wise to take final vows. Did I really want to—and was I able to—give up the prospect of marriage and children, not to mention other career options?

Realize that at this time in Church history, Catholic spirituality was often tainted with a fear-ridden and negative approach to human sexuality. In this puritanical climate, it was not uncommon to believe that one unguarded "impure thought" (any sexual fantasy was called an impure thought in those days) or pleasurable sensation could plunge you into mortal sin and, if you died in that state, eternal hellfire.

There is a humorous but true story about a grumpy old friar who lived at Duns Scotus at that time. He was known for his very negative and pessimistic view of human nature. One New Year's Eve, a student encountered the elderly friar hobbling down the corridor with his cane. "Happy New Year, Father, Happy New Year!" exclaimed the young friar, full of innocence and enthusiasm. The old friar turned scowling to the young Franciscan and grunted: "Bah—a lot of sins will be committed tonight!" Then with a "harumph" he went hobbling off again.

A puritan climate. During this era, it was standard for a religious manual to describe as an "ugly animal urge" what we would today call "healthy sexual impulses." One of the books recommended for novitiate reading had been

The Imitation of Christ, the fifteenth-century spiritual classic by Thomas á Kempis. Without denying *The Imitation*'s many positive contributions to the history of spiritual literature, it certainly had some negatives for us, at least, in the English translation used in 1955. In it we novices found human physical drives described as "evil passions" or "abominable fancies." At one point, the author pleads, "Good Jesus, ...fight strongly for me, vanquish these evil beasts—the alluring desires of the flesh."

True blessings and consolation, *The Imitation* added, are to be found "in contempt of all worldly things and in the cutting off of all base pleasures." One can hardly read the book without imbibing the dualistic viewpoint that spirit is good and human flesh is evil.

As far as my own personal battle with these "evil beasts" was concerned, I consulted several of our friar instructors—with great fear and trepidation. Was my seemingly endless struggle with these natural drives a sign I should leave the religious life? They all listened with respect, encouragement and brotherly concern, but ultimately without giving a clear direction or setting my heart at ease.

Peace of heart replaces anxiety. Finally, an older friar, Father Philibert Ramstetter—a seasoned spiritual adviser and philosopher, steeped in the best of the Franciscan tradition—gave me some wise and affirming counsel. Most of all, he said the words I most needed to hear, words that brought profound healing to my tortured heart: "Jack, you're not evil."

Our moments of greatest healing are also moments of light. Philibert, in a sense, had healed a disease of the eye by which I (and others of my era) saw only darkness where we should have seen light—namely, the light of God's goodness in the most intimate and innocent of our natural drives.

If there is anywhere that the light of the Creator needs to be recognized and admired, it is in the profound human impulse to find union with another and bring forth new life. To view this gift of life as an "evil beast" or "an ugly animal urge," as some spiritualities still put it, is truly a disease of the eye and a form of blasphemy. Jesus's words certainly apply here: "The eye is the lamp of the body. So, if your eye is healthy, your whole body will be full of light; but if your eye is unhealthy, your whole body will be full of darkness. If then the light in you is darkness, how great is the darkness!" (Matthew 6:22-23).

More and more, the insight grew in me that it was the God of light—certainly not the prince of darkness—who gave all women and men the yearning and capacity for loving physical union and the creation of new life. This is not to say, of course, that human beings cannot be corrupted or that they cannot use the powerful forces of nature in destructive and abusive ways. The story of creation, however, tells us these basic drives are "very good" when channeled in harmony with the Creator's plan and the welfare of humankind.

I remember finding additional comfort at the time from a quote from Bishop Fulton Sheen, a celebrated TV personality, speaker and popular spiritual writer during this era. His statement conveyed a beautiful image that helped assure me of the fundamental goodness of the wild forces within nature and within myself. To the best of my memory, Sheen's words went like this: "We admire a thundering cataract and a rushing river, not when they flood our farms or crush the flowers, but when they are harnessed to light a city or slake a child's thirst."

———————

PRAYER FOR A SOUND EYE

Loving Creator,
you are Father and Mother of us all.

Give healing to our eyes
that they may recognize your light and goodness
in our natural drives
and in every feature of our human form.

Your loving hands have made us
just the way we are.

Lead us to embrace completely
our human sexuality and gender
so that we may guide all our gifts
toward your service and the welfare of others. Amen.

The Word in Literature and Art

A NOTHER WELCOME STREAM of light during my Duns Scotus years emanated from Leander Blumlein, O.F.M., the friar-priest who made up the one-man literature department in our little liberal arts college. He had a profound influence on all of us by engendering in us an openness to the whole world of literature and art, music and cinema—not to mention philosophy, which formed the backbone of the curriculum.

Leander, who had received his graduate degree in literature from the University of Notre Dame under the influence of the famous Frank O'Mally, introduced his course each year by saying "Literature does not save the soul; it makes the soul worth saving." And week after week, we felt our souls being enriched and ennobled by the great poetry and novels and dramas we explored with him. He helped us find in the great works of literature and art the same mystery of God's goodness that Saint Francis saw behind the face of nature.

An attitude of reverence. Reverence born of a sense of

wonder was an attitude Leander helped us uncover in the writers and poets we studied. He also conveyed that spirit in his own teaching. Reverence, as he suggested, was a way of sitting down before truth like an innocent child. It was a way of responding to reality with wonder—a way of being open to mystery and respecting things, humbly, for what they were; not rushing in like know-it-alls and twisting the mysteries of life and nature to fit our own purposes.

He would gently point out this kind of reverence in the poetry of Robert Frost or in the essays of Emerson and Thoreau. For example, a two-line poem by Robert Frost entitled "The Secret Sits" captures well the spirit of reverence that Leander sought to convey:

> We dance round in a ring and suppose,
> But the secret sits in the middle and knows.

Presented here, rather coyly, is the idea that the profound inner meaning of things always remains hidden from us, no matter how often we circle around it and make bright guesses about its ultimate meaning. In everything, Frost seemed to sense an inexhaustible well of meaning and mystery which could never be completely plumbed.

To me, this is not many steps removed from the theme of this book, namely that the divine word sits mysteriously behind the created things of this world, giving all things a bottomless source of meaning and beauty. In his essay on "The Poet," Emerson shows himself pondering the same mystery. "A beauty not explicable," he writes, "is dearer than a beauty which we can see to the end of."

Although Emerson, to my knowledge, does not use the language of the Word of God as found in John's Gospel, he does speak in terms of the divine mind and the divine ideas. He sees the objects of the created world as emblems or symbols of a divine order that transcends this world. His premises and theology are obviously different from my own as a Catholic Christian, but I have always found his insights very illuminating—and quite adaptable to the Catholic vision.

An insight of Emerson which especially spoke to me during my years at Duns Scotus College was that of being true to one's own inner voice and to realize "that imitation is suicide." In Emerson's essay "Self-Reliance," I found encouragement to "trust thyself" and "speak your latent conviction." The implication was that divine wisdom reveals itself through our innermost thoughts and must be reverenced and not rejected. "A man should learn," writes Emerson, "to detect and watch that gleam of light which flashes across his mind from within...."

The quotation from "Self-Reliance" that I treasured more than others and reverently inscribed in my college notebook was: "We but half express ourselves, and are ashamed of the divine idea which each of us represents." From this insight, it was an easy step to the theology found in John's Gospel—to the belief that God's word is imprinted deep within each creature and within each human being. When you or I hear within our souls our own most authentic and honest voice, we are hearing the voice of God.

Pursuing a literary career. The influence of Leander was to shape my future in other ways, too. A few years down the road, his influence would lead me to pursue a master's degree in English literature.

After making my final vows as a Franciscan friar at Duns Scotus College chapel in 1958 and graduating in 1959, I moved, along with my class, to our theology school at St. Leonard College near Dayton, Ohio. In 1961, as a student there, I began spending summers in Cincinnati to study literature at Xavier University. Joining me in the same program was another theology student at St. Leonard's, longtime friend, Murray Bodo, who would become a well-known Franciscan author and poet.

I was ordained a Franciscan priest in 1963 at St. Leonard College, Murray the following year. I can't speak for Murray, but a question I found myself dealing with during this period was: How does the study of literature and the arts fit in with my pursuit of the religious and Franciscan life? Isn't this mixing of the secular and the sacred something of a contradiction?

A part of me understood that there was no real division between the secular and the sacred. There is only one world, and it is a holy world, because the word of God is present in all its parts and all its strivings. Anything that helps human beings develop to their full potential is holy.

I must be honest and say, however, that it took some time for me to be at peace with this viewpoint. Back at Duns Scotus College, Father Leander had done his best to help us see the sacred in the world of literature and art. In fact, I had responded wholeheartedly to his encouragement to get actively involved in the arts—to dabble in watercolors, woodcarving and silk-screening, theater, writing poetry and short stories. Yet some years passed before I became more fully comfortable with the vision that one's human development and spiritual development are the work of the same word. (The Church as a whole was beginning to formulate the same vision at the Second Vatican Council, 1962-1965.) The following poem, which I wrote in 1964, reflects my own struggle with this issue—and even suggests, happily, that I had come to a resolution.

An Apology for Artists

An old monk made some tiger cubs
from lumps of moldy clay,
then found a block of cherry wood
and gaily carved a tray.

His abbot caught him later still
with water paints and brush,
all smiles, and dabbing speckles
on a fresh and dazzling thrush.

"Jerome! Jerome!" the abbot cried,
"explain these vain distractions!
A monk should paint madonnas—
depict nice, pious actions."

"Well, tell me, sir," the monk replied,
while brushing off his habit,
"did God give you a good excuse
for making fox and rabbit?"

PRAYER TO HEAL DOUBLE VISION

Mysterious Source of all being,
help us to see that you alone are the one God
and there is no other—
even if we approach you by different paths.

And help us see that there is only one creation
and it is holy.

There are not two worlds:
a "holy" world and a "profane" world.
There is only one holy world.

It is our vision that is sometimes double.
Send us more light.
Make our vision one. Amen.

Saint Francis and the
Glory of Creation

T HE LOVE AND FASCINATION I had for nature as a
young boy in the Indiana woods stayed with me and
grew even stronger during my years as a Franciscan
student of philosophy and theology. I was always ready to
set aside my college texts and go enjoy the book of nature—
the trees and fields and brooks, the birds and other
creatures found in the wooded areas of the property
surrounding our seminaries in Michigan and Ohio.

Armed with binoculars and pocket manuals for
identifying birds and trees, I spent many hours taking
wide-eyed meditative walks through woods and field. At
our theology college near Dayton, Ohio, I joined two other
nature-loving friars, Bill Reichel and John Mittelstadt, in
building a bird blind deep in the woods with a large feeder
attached to the front of it.

We spent many a wintry afternoon in this crude hut,
observing at close range the antics of feathered sisters and
brothers. We even gave them humorous nicknames. The

little black-capped chickadees, for example, became "Freddy the Freeloaders" because they were always the first to fly in for the freebies. The nuthatches we called "technix" because of the technical precision with which they snatched and deftly maneuvered sunflower seeds in their beaks. Then there were the "Hoovers," our name for the slate-colored juncos. These determined little guys zoomed across the feeder floor like vacuum cleaners, snarfing up all the birdseed in their path! And so we passed the hours enjoying the antics of our sisters and brothers, the birds.

Francis and his unusual kinship with creatures. Perhaps my own attraction to nature made me curious about Saint Francis' habit of calling his fellow creatures "brother" and "sister." The little saint went happily about the Italian countryside, calling out with affection to "Brother Sun" and "Sister Moon," to "Brother Fire" and "Sister Water," to "Sister Swallow" and "Brother Cricket" and so forth.

What secret instinct or intuition, I wondered, led him to this easy, familial relationship with all creation? What fueled his vision of the universe as one happy, interconnected family? For years, I've been trying to come up with some answers to these questions.

First, I believe that Francis had an uncomplicated yet deep sense of the common goodness of creation because he saw it coming from the same good Creator. This, of course, made him a brother to all: If the marigold and the wolf had the same Father in heaven as he did, then quite simply, they were sister and brother to him.

More than this, it seems, the meaning of the Incarnation hit his imagination like a bombshell. Somehow he realized that when the Word entered the world of creation and became flesh, everything was profoundly changed. If God became a part of the created world in the birth of Jesus Christ, then the dignity of all creatures was raised dramatically to a new height. The original goodness of creation was reinforced a thousand times over when God waded into the stream of creation—into the realm of minerals and plants and animals, of snowflakes and rainstorms—and so entered the history of this planet!

To understand more fully Francis' instinct in this regard, we might go back and compare the ancient Greek view of physical matter with that of the Hebrew Scriptures. For some of the Greek philosophers, matter was seen as negative or evil, while spirit was always good. Matter was a prison of the spirit. It was matter, in their view, that kept us separated from each other and from union with God. When you and I die, we are freed from our chunk of inferior matter and our souls sail blissfully back into the ocean of spirit and unity.

This is not the Hebrew view of the material world. For them, flesh is good. It unifies and creates kinship among humans and other creatures. One Hebrew says to another: "Truly you are my flesh and bone." Indeed, Jesus reminded his audience of the words of Genesis that husband and wife "become one flesh" (see Genesis 2:24). We hear the psalmist inviting "all flesh" to bless the name of God (Psalm 145:21) and give thanks to God, "who gives food to all flesh" (Psalm 136:25).

Francis saw the world of matter and flesh in the same way—as if there is one stuff from which all things are made and which unites all creatures in solidarity, in one solid body of matter and flesh. Indeed, the Book of Genesis (2:9, 19) portrays God as making all eatthly things—plants, trees, animals, birds, human beings—from the same basic matter: out of the ground, dust or clay. Thus God made all of us creatures from the same stuff and "remembers that we are dust" (Psalm 103:14).

The Incarnation jolts the whole system. And Francis was deeply aware of one moment in history—the moment that God entered creation and the Word was made flesh. For Francis this event sent shock waves through the whole network of dust and flesh. Not only was human nature made holy by the Incarnation; the whole fabric of creation was also charged with the divine presence.

Francis sensed that all creation had been redeemed (not just humans) through the Incarnation. Did not John the Baptist proclaim in the words of Isaiah that "all flesh shall see the salvation of God" (Luke 3:6)? And did not Christ tell his followers to "proclaim the good news to the whole creation" (see Mark 16:15)? Why shouldn't Francis take this literally? Why shouldn't he preach to the birds and fishes and wolves? These are all part of the flesh, part of the brotherhood and sisterhood of creation. Francis refused to be a human chauvinist, pretending that he was saved apart from the rest of creation.

This is why the feast of Christmas meant so much to Francis and why he wanted the whole of creation to take part in the feast. In fact, history credits Francis of Assisi with beginning the tradition of the Christmas creche. This popular custom goes back to the year 1223, when Francis invited the townspeople of Greccio, Italy, to come to a cave outside town and reenact the first Christmas.

He instructed them to get ox and ass and sheep and real straw in a real manger. There is a legend that the Christ child appeared in the straw and Francis held the infant in his arms.

Nowhere in the Gospels does it say that an ox and ass were present at Christ's birth. The story simply comes from tradition or legend. Most of all, it comes from Francis' sense—or maybe a deep instinct in all of us—that all creatures, by right, participate in the celebration of Christmas.

Let heaven and nature sing! Francis' biographers go even further. They tell us that Francis, to extend the feast to all of nature, wanted the emperor to tell all citizens to scatter grain along the roads on Christmas day so that the birds and other animals would have plenty to eat. Walls, too, should be rubbed with meat, and the beasts in the stables should be given bounteous food as well.

I believe that you and I, though perhaps barely aware of it, harbor the same instinct as Francis. We too seek to include the whole of nature in our celebration of Christmas. Consider for a moment our Christmas tree custom. What are we really doing? We go out to the countryside (or, more likely, to the market) and get a tree. We bring this obvious symbol of creation into our homes and churches and decorate it beautifully during the Christmas season, covering it with strings of lights and lots of tinsel. Many of us, moreover, decorate the trees and shrubs in our yards—even our houses—with lights.

Unconsciously, are we not bringing "Brother Tree" and other parts of our world into our celebration of Christ's birth, our celebration of the entrance of God's Son into the created universe? Familiar Christmas carols like "Joy to the World" suggest that the whole earth is vibrating in harmony with the Good News of the Incarnation and resonating with our songs of praise. Indeed, as the popular carol puts it, "Fields and floods, rocks, hills and plains repeat the sounding joy."

If Francis were alive today, he would no doubt advise us to include more and more of creation in our celebration. He might even suggest that we put ribbons on Brother Dog and Sister Cat—or at least that we toss more seeds on the bird feeder on Christmas day. If he had enough lights, he would probably string them along our rivers and mountains and forests. "And look at the night sky," he would probably exclaim. "It is already covered with strings of shining stars!"

PRAYER TO FIND GOD'S GLORY IN CREATURES

Word of God,
you once walked this planet
as brother to birds and flowers and trees,

to deserts and lakes,
to the sun and moon and stars,
as well as to human beings.

You became part of the network of creation,
revealing to creation its own glorious dignity.

Help us to grow,
like Saint Francis,
in our oneness with you
and with all flesh. Amen.

Christ, the Head of Creation

I HOPE YOU ARE WILLING to plunge a little deeper into the Franciscan vision of the created universe. In the Franciscan way of thinking, Jesus Christ, the Word made flesh, is not simply a part of creation. Christ is the final goal and summit toward which all creation is headed.

A key point of the Franciscan view that is often surprising to some is this: The Word of God did not become a creature, a human being, because Adam and Eve sinned. Rather, the divine Word became flesh because from all eternity God wanted Christ to be creation's most perfect work, the model and crown of creation and of humanity—the glorious destination toward which all creation is straining. The Word would have been incarnated in Christ even if the first man and woman had never sinned!

The foremost champion of these views—after Saint Paul, of course, whose writings first introduced them— was the Franciscan friar Blessed John Duns Scotus. Scotus was born in Scotland in 1266, educated at England's Oxford University and ordained a Franciscan priest in

1291. He taught theology at the University of Paris and in 1308 was buried in Cologne, Germany, where he died at forty-two. Though the approach of John Duns Scotus differs from that of standard Catholic theology, it has never been labeled unacceptable by the Church. And Franciscans, over the centuries, have generally imbibed Scotus' way of looking at Christ.

If anything, Scotus' viewpoint has gained prominence in recent times. It has been adopted by such notable Catholic thinkers as Gerard Manley Hopkins, the Jesuit poet; Thomas Merton, the Trappist writer; and Teilhard de Chardin, the Jesuit priest-anthropologist. "Christ is not an afterthought in the divine plan," writes de Chardin. "He is the Alpha and the Omega, the beginning and the end of all things."

Moreover, the beatification of John Duns Scotus by Pope John Paul II in 1993 can be seen as a belated vote of confidence by the Church regarding the holiness and virtue of John Duns Scotus—as well as his theological contributions.

According to Scotus, God's first intention—from all eternity—was that human nature be glorified by being united to the divine Word. And this was to happen *regardless* of the first humans' innocence or sinfulness. To say that the Incarnation of Christ was an afterthought of God, dependent on Adam's fall, would be to base the rich Christian theology of Incarnation on sin! Theologians could come up with something better than that, and Duns Scotus did.

Of course, given humanity's sin, the *way* Christ

eventually came was in the form of a Savior whose great act of love and self-surrender set us free. In Scotus' view, however, the God-man would have entered creation and human history under any circumstances as the perfect model of the human being fully alive. It was not Adam who provided the blueprint or pattern that God used in shaping the humanity of Christ. It was the other way around, insists Scotus: Christ was the model in God's mind according to which Adam and Eve, as well as the rest of the human race, were created.

Created in Christ's image. Francis of Assisi, whose vision always centered on Christ, provided a foundation upon which the later Franciscan vision or school of thought would be built. "Be conscious, O human being," Francis wrote in his *Admonitions*, "of the wondrous state in which the Lord God has placed you, for he created you and formed you to the image of his beloved Son."

But the Letters of Saint Paul already contained a basis for seeing Christ as the summit and pattern for all of creation. Paul tells the Ephesians:

> [God] chose us in Christ,
> before the world was made
> to be holy and faultless before him in love....
> Such was his purpose and good pleasure,
> to the praise of the glory of his grace,
> his free gift to us in the Beloved,..."
> (Ephesians 1:4, 6, *New Jerusalem Bible*).

Then, in Ephesians 1:10 (*New Jerusalem Bible*), comes Paul's magnificent description of God's plan

> ...when the times had run their course:
> that he would bring everything together under Christ, as head,
> everything in the heavens and everything on earth.

In Colossians we read Paul's most celebrated passage about what many call the "primacy of Christ"—his having first place and being the central focus in God's plan for creation: "[Christ] is the image of the invisible God, the firstborn of all creation; for in him all things in heaven and on earth were created, things visible and invisible...all things have been created through him and for him. He himself is before all things, and in him all things hold together" (Colossians 1:15-17).

Franciscans and the "primacy of Christ." Most Franciscans, I believe, have in one way or another embraced this vision. Whether conscious of it or not, they tend to see all created things as pieces of a beautiful puzzle that only make sense when fitted into the larger framework—the image of Christ.

For several years, I've kept in my cassette collection an audiotape on the letters to the Ephesians and Colossians by Father Stephen Doyle, O.F.M., a well-known Franciscan Scripture scholar and popular preacher. I have often listened to this tape because I find it an engaging explanation of the Franciscan/Scotist approach to the primacy of Christ without even mentioning Scotus or the

Franciscan tradition. Franciscan spirituality just exudes naturally from this friar as he talks about Paul's view of Christ, "the firstborn of all creation."

Throughout this talk, Father Stephen smuggles in such little comments as "There is nothing in this world that makes sense apart from Jesus Christ" and "Whatever exists in this world was made for the sake of Jesus Christ." Later, he waxes poetic: "If we looked around and listened to this world about us, and if the singing birds could be formed into a chorus and the rustling breeze and tinkling rain could have a voice and the roar of the ocean could be put into words, they would all have one thing to say: 'We were made for the sake of Jesus Christ.' "

Father Stephen also offers a good answer to the riddle: How can it be that Christ, who came *after* Adam and Eve, nonetheless came *before* them in God's thinking? How can the Incarnate Word be the first and the last at the same time? Borrowing a popular analogy found in Saint Francis de Sales' *Treatise on the Love of God*, Father Stephen explains it this way:

> If you wanted to make wine, what would you do? First of all, you would have to plant a vineyard. Then you would have to fertilize the vines. You would have to trim them. Eventually, you would harvest the grapes, press them and let them ferment. Finally, you would get some wine.
>
> What was the first thing on your mind? The wine. What was the last thing you got? The wine.

In the same way, Jesus' arriving late on the scene, notes Father Stephen, does not contradict his holding first place in God's mind at the creation of the universe. Christ is the first and the last, the Alpha and the Omega.

Christ is the key—the measure of humanity. Meister Eckhart, a medieval Dominican theologian who died in 1327, affirmed that there was only "one word" spoken by the Father, namely, the Son of God. "And in that single Word, God uttered all things."

This teaching helps us realize that all of Scripture, though composed of many words, characters and actions, is leading up to and giving shape and expression to the *one Word* of God, whom we Christians profess as Jesus Christ, the Word made flesh.

Similarly, in the ongoing process of creation and human history itself, there are many elements: minerals, plants, animals, human characters. Yet in the Christian view, as Saint Paul expresses so well, all these elements and characters are coming to a culmination in Jesus Christ. God's plan, we recall, is to "bring everything together under Christ, as head" (see Ephesians 1:10).

It is as though all of us play a part in that one sacred Word, that one mysterious drama of love, present in the mind of God from all eternity. The thought is awesome— a beauty whose end we cannot see. Starting with the first day of creation, the Word of God—the coeternal mirror of the Father—has been slowly emerging down the ages. This Word has become visible in the Incarnation and will reach its full revelation when Jesus returns in glory on the last day.

We, too, are part of the Word made flesh by grace and adoption, to use Saint Paul's expression. We, too, are members of the Body of Christ, with Christ as head. Along with the whole of creation, we are given a role in the emerging of the one Word.

I have found in the writings of Pope John Paul II some hints that his thinking resonates well with the "primacy of Christ" doctrine and other elements in Saint Paul's vision of creation. He certainly sees Christ as the primary key to understanding the universe and as the model and measure against which human beings can assess their own meaning, value and success. In short, Christ is the one who sheds light on our meaning and the destiny of the universe.

In his encyclical *Redeemer of the Human Race* the pope proclaims: "Jesus is the center of the universe and of history" (#1). Later he adds, "Christ the Redeemer 'fully reveals human beings to themselves' " and "if we wish to understand ourselves thoroughly,...we must draw near to Christ.... In Christ and through Christ, human persons have acquired full awareness of their dignity, of the heights to which they are raised, of the surpassing worth of their humanity, and of the meaning of existence" (#10, 11).

Christ's final bow on history's stage. Some years ago I attended a stage play. During the final curtain call an intuition flashed into my mind. It struck me that what was happening on that stage was a shadowy image of what will happen at the end of the larger drama of history itself.

We know well the ritual at the end of a stage play.

When the curtain reopens, we once again see the familiar set and furnishings, the "world" of the drama just presented. Then all the characters, from the lesser to the greater, begin coming on to the stage. All have been a part of this one dramatic story, this "one word" or "conception" expressing the mind and heart of the author. The performers continue to fill up the stage until at the very end, as the lights grow brighter and the applause grows louder, the star of the show—glowing in the light—comes forward to take the final bow.

We can look at the drama of history and salvation in the same way. All of us humans, with our fellow creatures of all the centuries, have been offered a role to play in the drama, *Word Becoming Flesh*. When the drama ends, we will all have a chance to take our little bows and then turn to await the reentrance of the lead player, Jesus Christ, the head of creation, the final judge and measure of what it means to be truly human. As he comes back on stage to take his final bow, the lights grow brighter, and the praise from the whole audience of creation is deafening.

PRAYER TO THE DIVINE WORD

O Divine Word,
we listen to your voice
embedded deep within us,
within nature and, of course,
revealed in Scripture

and, most eminently,
in the Word made flesh.

May you lead us
to the full measure of creaturehood
we are meant to become,
the very stature of Christ.

Guide us forward to this,
our glorious destiny. Amen.

A New Dawn of Liberation

O N JUNE 13, 1963, along with the eight other friars in my class, I was ordained a Franciscan priest at St. Leonard College near Dayton, Ohio. Later that year, we moved to Louisville, Kentucky, to take part in a pastoral training program that lasted several months. A memorable experience during that time was taking part in a civil rights march led by Martin Luther King, Jr.

Together with a group of lay Franciscans from Louisville, we friars went to Frankfort, the state capital, to participate in this event. The march ended with a speech delivered by Dr. King to a large crowd of listeners standing patiently in a wintry drizzle. I still have a photo that I took of Dr. King as he gave his speech while an aide held an umbrella over his head.

Something King said on that occasion brought sudden illumination to me and sticks in my memory: "The law can't make a man love me," he told the crowd, "but it can keep him from lynching me!"

King's perspective and his whole movement of nonviolent social activism represent for me one of the great moments of light in the twentieth century. With incisive comments like the one above, King helped his generation to see that the Christian mission is not only to change the sinful attitudes in the human heart. Our mission is also to change the sinful legal structures and customs of society that oppress people. The vision of Martin Luther King helped to bring about a new dawn of human liberation.

Change social structures as well as hearts. Up to this point, many Christians believed that the single aim of evangelization was to "save souls" or convert human hearts. To change laws and practices that hold certain races or classes in bondage was not part of the Christian concern, according to this view. Consequently, the Church should stay out of politics. And those suffering oppression in this life should just be patient: In the next life, they will be set free of their misery.

King and his supporters, however, did not agree. They could no longer tolerate the social structures, laws and customs that forced black citizens to sit in the back of buses and stay away from "whites only" drinking fountains, swimming pools, lunch counters, schools, and so on. They insisted that the task of Christianity included the elimination of all forms of social evil that affront the dignity of human beings created in God's image.

Jesus—a model for setting humanity free. Martin Luther King's viewpoint flowed directly from the gospel and our whole Judeo-Christian tradition. Jesus clearly saw his task and that of his disciples as one of setting men and women free not only of personal sin but also of everything that hindered their full human development as children of God.

At the beginning of his ministry, Jesus described his mission by boldly reading from Isaiah the prophet in the synagogue at Nazareth:

> The Spirit of the Lord is upon me,
>   because he has anointed me
>   to bring good news to the poor.
> He has sent me to proclaim release to the captives
>   and recovery of sight to the blind,
>   to let the oppressed go free...." (Luke 4:18-19)

Jesus did not act in a vacuum. He was part of a long tradition established by Moses and the Hebrew prophets. Moses, for example, already stood for centuries as a great model of liberation. From the burning bush, Moses had been called by Yahweh to set a captive people free. "The cry of the Israelites has now come to me," [Yahweh told him]; "I have also seen how the Egyptians oppress them. So come, I will send you to Pharaoh to bring my people, the Israelites, out of Egypt" (Exodus 3:9-10).

In recent decades, we have been returning to a more integral view of salvation that is part and parcel of the biblical tradition. God's plan is not simply to get souls to heaven, but also to bring salvation to the whole human enterprise, beginning right here on earth. President John F. Kennedy, who was assassinated within a month or so of Martin Luther King's speech, put it this way in his 1961 inaugural address: "Here on earth God's work must truly be our own."

All human beings, therefore, are called to be prophets: to help rid the world of every form of slavery and sin—whether that sin be personal or social. Social sins that especially need to be exposed to the light and uprooted are racism and sexism—and all other "isms" that dehumanize sisters and brothers.

At the 1971 World Synod of Bishops in Rome, the Roman Catholic community reached a flash point of understanding regarding its own prophetic mission. In their statement, *Justice in the World*, the bishops declared: "Action on behalf of justice and participation in the transformation of the world fully appear to us as an essential dimension of the preaching of the gospel."

Such statements of principle from on high, of course, have to be translated to the level of everyday behavior. We must make applications in our homes and streets and workplaces. The challenge is not only for those in Congress or city hall but for everyone, including those sitting around the kitchen table! There, for example, one has daily opportunities to remind and challenge children and loved ones to avoid racist or sexist remarks and to treat all with respect.

————————

PRAYER FOR PROPHETIC COURAGE

*O God, liberator of the oppressed,
show us how to participate*

in your work of helping people everywhere
reach their full freedom and humanity.

Give us the light to see
that no individual does the work of justice alone—
nor can we do it alone—
but only as instruments of your power and love,
which always accompany us. Amen.

Light in the Philippines

A FTER COMPLETING the pastoral training program in Louisville in 1964, I moved to Cincinnati to begin my first full-time assignment as a Franciscan friar. For one year, I was an English, journalism and religion teacher at Roger Bacon High School in Cincinnati. Then I moved to Fort Wayne, Indiana, and for the next four years taught English at another school of ours, Bishop Luers High School. On weekends I helped out at local parish churches. Though I found high school teaching difficult and emotionally demanding, I liked the students a lot, became quite content with my career and established close friendships inside and outside the school.

Then one day in 1968, out of the blue, I got a phone call from Father Mel Brady, O.F.M., a former seminary teacher of mine who was now rector of a Franciscan college seminary just outside Manila in the Philippine islands. The phone call would mark a surprising detour in my life journey—a detour that would lead me down a path of unexpected light.

Mel asked if I would consider coming to the Philippines

for two or three years to teach English to Filipino Franciscan seminarians. I told him I was willing to come if needed. I discussed the idea of going to the Philippines with my Franciscan provincial in Cincinnati. After some dialogue, he suggested that I would get the go-ahead if I put my request for this foreign assignment in writing.

One day, as I was giving this option serious thought while praying alone in the friary chapel at Bishop Luers, I suddenly began weeping. The tears came partly because my heart knew I had come to a "yes" in the face of what seemed—to me, at least—a major, life-changing call. But there was more than anguish in the weeping. There was joy and light, too. For I sensed, even then, that my decision was more God's gift to me than my gift to God and to whomever I might serve in the Philippines.

The decision, of course, was not without the usual mixture of motives. The opportunity to travel to new lands and cultures was certainly an attractive prospect to me. But I was also aware of my own limitations. Obviously, I would carry with me to the Philippines my own cultural and personal baggage, my own frailty and personal shortcomings.

In any event, I made the decision. And in the summer of 1969, after saying my goodbyes, I flew to the Philippine islands.

An explosion of light. The greatest blessing I experienced in the Philippines, besides the love of its people, was the blessing of light. In so many ways my mind was pried open, stretched and filled with new understanding and insights. There was no avoiding the cross-cultural bombardment that shook my vision and turned many of my North American standards on their heads.

I went to the Philippines to be an educator of young Filipino men who had came to our seminary to become Franciscan friars. In reality, these native students, who often came from the country's remote islands, were *my* educators. In addition, just being part of an international Franciscan faculty, composed of Spaniards, Italians, Australians, Filipinos, a Croatian and other Americans— each with their own viewpoints and agendas—was itself an eye-opening, mind-stretching experience.

I discovered that I had really not had a clear sense of my own cultural identity as an American and a Westerner. But when my cultural viewpoints began bumping against those of the Asians and my international colleagues, I started to see better my own national definition and cultural biases. Then, too, I could not help seeing all about me the effects of Western colonialism upon this society, which for centuries had lived under the sway of Spain and, more recently, of the United States.

One of the greatest gifts I received during my three-year stay in the Philippines was the display of love, hospitality, laughter and warmth that is so typical of the Philippine people. When I went to celebrate Mass in the barrios or visit families and friends or meet with students and coworkers at the seminary or at Maryknoll Women's College (where I also taught literature), people always had time for me and were most personable and cordial.

Social events did not always start on time because

people and their needs were always more important than schedules or the job at hand. This made me realize how task-oriented and time-conscious—and often impersonal—Americans can be by contrast. I began to discover how I, as an American, was always so serious about checking my watch and getting down to business. The Filipinos were the first to teach me the meaning of the Oriental expression: "We don't have watches; we have time." They taught me to lighten up and laugh and take time for human interchange and affection.

Comparing Asian and American values. After my first year of teaching at Our Lady of the Angels, I was asked to be chaplain for a small group of Franciscan college students who were going to Cebu City, the Philippines' second largest city. These students would be taking summer courses at the University of San Carlos in that bustling port city, situated on the island of Cebu.

This gave me the opportunity to take some classes myself at that university. One of the classes was Filipino Literature in English, a course that was itself an insightful journey into the Filipino culture. (I would be teaching it myself the next semester back at the seminary. There I would have the perfect opportunity to learn about the culture from students who grew up in it.) The other was Filipino Values, taught by Doctor Lourdes Quisumbing, a well-known sociologist who later became Secretary of Education for the Philippines under President Corazon Aquino.

Doctor Quisumbing's class was largely a comparison of

Asian-Filipino cultural values with those of the United States. I found her course spellbinding. Scales seemed to fall from my eyes as she explained the different sets of presumptions upon which American and Filipino approaches to life were based.

To give just one example, Doctor Quisumbing explained that in the Philippine culture—and in Asia generally—people grow up learning to face life together. Families are close-knit. They are expected to be emotionally interdependent—to meet life's problems as a social unit. American culture, on the other hand, typically teaches its children to become emotionally independent as early as possible, so individuals can face life's difficulties on their own. The American ideal is to prevail on your own—like so many of the heroes in our movies.

How true this rang to me! As I grew up in the United States, I was seldom pampered by parents, relatives or teachers. Theirs was a kind of tough love that taught me to face life with a stiff upper lip. I learned rather early to go hunting and fishing by myself. In U.S. society it would not seem strange for me to go to the swimming pool or gym to work out on my own. There were frequently times in the Philippines, however, when I went somewhere on my own and was asked, "Where is your companion?" The cultural assumption behind the question was that human beings should be facing life together, not alone.

Thus my Philippine experience was teaching me to test and question my own cultural presuppositions. I actually learned to be less of a loner, to be more personable and openly affectionate and to see the value of family closeness and emotional support. I saw how the Philippine approach reflected the Christian ideal of being one Body and bearing one another's burdens. At the same time, I could still see the need for emotional independence, such as that independence exhibited by the prophets and Jesus when they had to stand up against the crowd, even when abandoned by their own.

Without judging, Doctor Quisumbing gave a multitude of examples of how American and Asian perspectives differ. Day after day this great teacher enlarged our cultural vision and understanding. She taught us, above all, to revere the different ways of the earth's peoples. "To judge other cultures by your standards is *insult*," she used to say. "To judge them by their standards is *insight*."

Other memories and goodbyes. I experienced both hardships and blessings during my three-year stint in the Philippines. Among the blessings, certainly, was the friendship and love of many Franciscan brothers and sisters, native Filipinos as well as colleagues from other countries.

One American friar, Father Max Hottle, O.F.M., of the California Franciscans, and I became fast friends and confidants. We were roughly the same age and of the same mischievous temperament. Max had a head start on me in understanding the cultural background of the Philippines. Trained in sociology at Manila's Jesuit university, he had already been teaching social studies at the seminary for several years before I arrived. His often humorous and wry observations were always full of light, wit and fraternal warmth and were a medicine for my soul.

One of the highlights of our camaraderie was taking a motorbike vacation in the summer of 1971 through the mountains of Luzon to visit the famous Banawe rice terraces and other wonderful places. We fancied ourselves Asia's answer to the American movie *Easy Rider*, a big hit all around the world at the time. The image of the film's two hippies on motorbike quickly became the running joke of our adventures!

As I look back on my time in Asia, I see it as a gift of Providence and a preparation for my future work as a writer and editor with an interest in global issues. High on the list of things I discovered in the Philippines was this: *Cross-cultural experience* is another word for light.

Even before I went to the Philippines and was wondering, with some trepidation, what the future would bring, I had latched on to Psalm 121 as a consoling prayer for God's protection. It often brought me comfort in my wanderings so far from home. Here is an abridged and adapted version of that psalm for all those who are anxious about what is coming next in their life's journey. It's also my prayer that God may always be your constant traveling companion:

Your Guardian Never Sleeps

God will not suffer your foot to slip;
for the God who guards you does not slumber.

The guardian of Israel
neither slumbers nor sleeps.

The Lord is your guardian and your shade—
a faithful protector at your side.

The sun shall not harm you by day,
nor the moon by night.

God will guard you from all evil;
God will guard your life.

God will guard your coming and your going
both now and forever.

———————

PRAYER FOR OPENNESS

God of all nations,
do not slumber
in your love for the Philippines
and all the peoples of the earth.

Forgive the sins that we,
shaped by different cultures,
commit against each other
through ignorance, weakness and inexperience.

Fill us with your all-embracing love and goodness
that we may carry your kind of love
to all races and peoples. Amen.

The Long Way Home

I LEFT THE PHILIPPINES with mixed feelings. It was difficult leaving a country that had given me so much and separating from friends whom I had come to love. On the other hand, I was looking forward to reuniting with family and friends in the United States after a three-year absence. I was also eager to begin a new phase in my Franciscan journey as a writer and religious journalist.

Well, being a writer was not entirely new. As a student, I had always been attracted—if not driven—to write for our Franciscan seminary publications. I had also studied creative writing at the University of Louisville and Notre Dame and journalism one summer at Marquette. I had even experienced the excitement of seeing a few free-lance articles of mine appear in Catholic magazines, including *St. Anthony Messenger*, a national magazine published by my Franciscan province in Cincinnati.

In fact, during my last year in the Philippines, I had written an article for that publication on Pope Paul VI's 1971 visit to Manila and the state of the Church in that country. The magazine's young, visionary editor at the time was Father Jeremy Harrington, O.F.M., whom I knew personally, a fellow Franciscan of the Cincinnati province. He wrote me a few months before I was to finish my time in the Philippines and invited me to join the staff of *St. Anthony Messenger*. It all seemed providential.

The journey home. The pain of leaving the Philippines was also muted by the excitement of the long trip home with stops in Thailand, India, the Holy Land, Greece, Italy, Austria, Germany, Spain, France, England and Ireland. The trip was exciting. Enough soul-expanding things happened to fill a book, but this is not that book. I will just share one little out-of-the-way incident from that trip which had a special impact on me. It took place at the Shrine of Our Lady in Lourdes, France. From my earliest years as a Roman Catholic, I had heard about this famous shrine and was drawn to it as toward a magnet.

As a young boy, I had seen the movie *Song of Bernadette*, which dramatized the appearances of the Virgin Mary at Lourdes. I still remember the scene where the young visionary, Bernadette, digs into the ground at the Lady's instruction only to see a miraculous spring of water issue forth.

A few weeks before my stop at Lourdes, a Catholic traveler told me to be sure to take in the bathing pools at the shrine. I had thought that only people with serious illness or disabilities were lowered into the spring-fed pools in the hope of being cured. "No," she told me, "every visitor should experience these baths."

My first night at Lourdes, I felt like a lonely pilgrim

reaching out for the healing presence of Mother Mary's love. What I was yearning for, I believe, and somehow sensed there in the darkness, was the maternal love of God, such as Yahweh promised through Isaiah: "As a mother comforts her child,/so I will comfort you" (Isaiah 66:13a). I had always seen such love embodied in Mary, whom Catholics revere as the Mother of God and the Mother of the Church.

It was damp, cold and drizzly the next morning when I went to the shrine's bathing pools. An attendant kindly showed me to a small dressing room next to one of the pools where I could remove my clothes and wrap around my waist the denim cloth they handed me. Two attendants greeted me at the pool. The water, which came up to my knees, was cold. After reciting a gentle prayer, they carefully lowered me, back first, into the water. I expected the water to feel shockingly cold, but it seemed remarkably comfortable. They helped me stand up again and led me dripping out of the pool.

I was invited to get dressed and leave. It was not necessary to dry off, they told me. My clothes would not get wet. Strangely enough, after I got dressed, my clothes seemed perfectly dry. On more than one occasion since that event, other visitors to Lourdes shared with me this same experience of their clothes not getting wet.

But that is not my most vibrant memory of the experience. I can't explain it, but after I got dressed and was walking away from the baths, I had an amazing feeling of innocence and new life. It was as if I was cleansed of all my sins. I felt whiter than snow! Although this experience happened more than twenty-three years ago, it remains as fresh in my memory as if it just happened yesterday. It was an inexplicable moment of light.

Whatever mixed feelings I still had about leaving the Philippines, whatever darkness or failure or guilt I felt in my heart, they were now replaced by healing and light—at least for the time being. I felt like a little child whose bruises or hurts had been kissed by an unseen yet loving Mother. I was suddenly healed, and ready to resume my journey with a lighter step.

Home—but not really home. I arrived back in the United States in the middle of the summer, 1972. I was home again. But I did not really feel at home. Yes, I felt happy to be reunited with family and friends. It was exciting visiting the offices at *St. Anthony Messenger* in downtown Cincinnati, meeting the staff and seeing my new work space. I had an inkling that I had found the right niche for myself and that I would ultimately be very happy in this new world of religious journalism.

Deep inside, however, I felt lost and broken. I had entered a dark place of emotional pain which, I suppose, had been put on hold during my meandering trip home as I moved from one distraction to another. Now I felt alienated from myself. Though I could enjoy my assignments, I felt that a core part of me was just going through empty motions.

A strong image kept coming back to me as a symbol of my emotional state at the time. It was the image of my heart as a broken stained-glass window. Though once standing secure and glowing with light, or so I thought, it now lay shattered and spread out in dark pieces on the cold ground. My identity seemed fallen apart, with no comfort in sight.

For one thing, I was suffering what they call "reverse culture shock." I was no longer the same person who left the States three years earlier. My perspectives and identity had changed because of my Asian experience. I did not feel fully at home in my own culture.

I had also imbibed, I believe, the turmoil of a Catholic Church still rocking in the wake of the Second Vatican Council. The roles of religious men and women were evolving. Priests and sisters were leaving their religious communities to get married. Church rituals, traditions and outlooks were changing. All the familiar points of reference were gone.

Most of all, perhaps, I felt cut off and so far away from the love and support I had come to know from dear friends in the Philippines. On the American side, too, I felt abandoned by a special friend who I thought would be an emotional stay for me. My heart and self-esteem felt crushed and battered.

Sources of comfort and light. Fortunately, I could pour out my heartache and confusion before my confrere and confidant, Murray Bodo, whose wise and brotherly affirmation has always been a healing balm. Behind a mask of nonchalance, I carried on. Day after day, however, I kept tasting my cup of darkness and brokenness.

Somehow, I clung to the Good News that light and

goodness are the ultimate reality, not darkness. Despite my pain I found joy in my writing, support in my Franciscan community as well as from coworkers, friends old and new, and family. I had to trust—on blind faith—that God's light and goodness were still there above the dark fog surrounding my soul. Some day the fog would lift and the light would break through.

I recall finding light in the words of various authors and friends who seemed able to pluck hope from the ashes of suffering. I took heart, for example, in a line remembered from Ernest Hemingway. He had written somewhere that broken hearts are like broken bones: They get stronger in the broken places.

A quote in a letter from a dear friend in the Philippines also offered me the kind of light and comfort that helps one carry on: "Our human choice is not between pain and no pain," she wrote, "but between the pain of loving and the pain of not loving." I found hope in her caring words and in the truth they conveyed: As human beings we are not always free to escape suffering, but we are free to take a stand toward that suffering.

Like my dear friend, I, too, wanted to make my pain a "pain of loving," which alone can give it meaning. On the other hand, nothing seemed worse to me than to choose "the pain of not loving," that is, to undergo pain without any love or meaning in sight.

Another quotation that testified to the existence of hope in the dark pit of suffering was that of French writer Leon Bloy: "There are places in the human heart which do not yet exist, and into them enters suffering that they may have existence." Bloy's words helped me to hold on to the Christian belief that suffering can be redemptive.

As a matter of fact, I found that in time something good did come from the suffering. My own pain and brokenness had given birth to new places of feeling within me—to new depths of compassion and sensitivity for others who suffer. I felt a new solidarity with struggling humanity and with all living things. I understood better what the poet Wordsworth meant when, after going through severe grief over the death of his sister, he said: "A deep distress has humanized my soul."

Finally, after about a year, my heart began to heal and be at peace. The pain, for the most part, had ebbed away. And those pieces of broken stained glass spread out on the cold, cold ground—what about them? Somehow, through the goodness of God, they quite mysteriously all came back together in a newly integrated whole.

To reach this new integration, however, it seemed that the old window and its frame had to break—no matter what the trauma or pain. But now the mended pieces and the new window that replaced it were larger than before— and the Light that shone through it now seemed to have a richer, warmer glow. It was the summer of 1973. I had finally come home!

Prayer to Find Peace in God

Loving God,
you are Mother and Father to us.

In you alone is our soul at rest.
As Augustine says, "You have made us for yourself,
and our heart is restless until it rests in you."

We come to you in moments of brokenness,
seeking comfort and healing,
because you who invite us
are the doctor of our souls. Amen.

Resurrection

T HAT SUMMER OF HEALING, I remember thinking
that I had experienced a rising from the grave. I had
been dead—emotionally—and now I was walking in the
light of a new day that felt fresher and more wonderful
than anything I had known before. In my very bones I *knew*
the resurrection. I could believe a bit more easily this
doctrine of my Christian faith.

Attending classes at the Jesuit-run University of San
Francisco that summer of 1973 greatly helped my healing
process. The magical atmosphere of that city by the bay
named after Saint Francis of Assisi was itself an elixir.
More than that, the refresher courses I took in religious
education allowed me to breathe in the new spirit of the
Second Vatican Council. The buoyant liturgies and the
compassionate friends I met that summer were also
encounters with hope and with the healing light of God's
love.

The joy of journalism. At the same time, I was finding new
life and excitement in writing articles for *St. Anthony*

Messenger. It was dawning on me that I had found my true avocation and mission in the arena of popular print communications.

Doing interviews was especially appealing. Time and again it struck me that the seeds of God's word and of God's light grow deep inside each human being. The interviewer's task, it seemed to me, was to try to draw forth that light. Without fail, I saw in the people I interviewed— no matter what their persuasion—a readiness to tap their deepest human and spiritual resources and share the light they found within.

Often these people were neither theologians or saints, but each in her or his own way was in touch with God's light within. Here are five brief examples from the hundreds of people I have interviewed over the years. I chose these five personalities because they may be people you already know.

A new look at death and dying. One of the first people I ever interviewed was Elisabeth Kübler-Ross, psychiatrist and author of the ground-breaking 1969 best-seller, *On Death and Dying*. We talked together in her then home just outside Chicago on a snowy March evening in 1973.

The key point of light Dr. Ross shared was this: When you get close to and identify with suffering and dying people, you are able to "go through the stages of suffering with them." And this ultimately benefits you. "Each time you can accept another's death," she said, "you come closer to accepting your own death. That is the gift that dying people give you if you dare to get involved with them." And we are not doing our children a favor, she insisted, when we shield them from all contact with suffering and death.

Describing herself as Swiss Protestant in background, Dr. Ross praised Catholics for having a sacrament—the Anointing of the Sick—that faces the fact of sickness and death. "Catholics," she noted, "are the only people I know who have a ritual that accepts the fact of death and have the courage to face it."

When asked how she felt about Francis of Assisi's calling out to his own approaching death as "Sister Death"—as if death were an old friend—Dr. Ross responded: "I feel like a related soul!"

Can Archie Bunker be saved? A few months later, actor Carroll O'Connor agreed to be interviewed in Los Angeles. O'Connor was playing the role of Archie Bunker in the TV comedy hit *All in the Family*—one of the hottest shows on TV, watched by an estimated fifty million Americans every Saturday night.

In an interview over lunch at the Beverly Hills Hotel in June 1973, O'Connor discussed the bigotry and racism displayed by Archie Bunker. By lampooning Archie's prejudices, he thought, the show was exposing the biases of our society and perhaps satirizing them out of existence.

O'Connor shared several illuminating insights about the way we humans develop prejudice at an early age. "Bigotry is a trap," said O'Connor. "Children are thrown into that trap at a very early age. Parents tell them that they can't play with certain children or they make disparaging remarks about Jewish kids.... A child at that age believes anything his parents tell him. And it's a *loving* mother or father that misleads him, so the innocent child is in a trap encased in love."

Prejudice towards blacks, too, is smuggled into a child's awareness side by side with parental love. "And it's love that makes it indelible," insists O'Connor, "because a rejection of our parents' ideas seems to be a rejection of the love that accompanies those ideas. One doesn't want to say, 'My mother was all wrong,' so the growing child goes on with the mother's ideas—out of love."

We have to forgive people like Archie, O'Connor suggested, because his fundamental errors are things he inherited unconsciously. "I don't dislike Archie Bunker. I feel very sorry for him and for his errors." O'Connor held out the hope that the Archie Bunkers of the world could be saved if the Churches and others could be understanding toward them and yet challenge them to see their blind spots. O'Connor saw even in Archie "something we call grace—a light that glows dimly" in his soul.

The actor. Actor Martin Sheen, in an interview in Studio City, California, in 1979, spoke about a holy presence within the human. Sheen didn't use the word *light* exactly, but spoke rather of the "sacredness" within. He had just completed working on his leading role in the Francis Ford Coppola film *Apocalypse Now*, which was about to be released.

Sheen said acting was a sacred profession because actors come into close contact with the creative energy of

God. "The secret of good acting," he said, "is not getting into someone else's feeling. It's getting into my own. To be a good actor, you just have to be aware of areas within yourself—either explored or unexplored—that you are now going to tap. And that's where the sacredness comes from. For now I'm going into the valley of my deepest feelings. I'm going to explore something I'm not permitted to do out there [in everyday life], but I can explore it in here as an actor.... It's a very sacred area.

"My role as an actor is not that different from yours as a priest," he insisted. "The only thing I can compare acting to is a church or a temple.... To me, acting is a very, very sacred thing.... Every time I walk on a set or a stage, it's my church and a sacred kind of thing is happening."

The dancer. The following year, 1980, actor Gene Kelly shared a bit of his spiritual journey in his home in Beverly Hills. Kelly said that human beings have to hold on to joy even in the face of adversity. "You can't mope around," he said. Even when it rains, you have to focus on the light and not the darkness. "Cheerfulness and good humor have always been important values for me," Kelly affirmed. "Gloom doesn't help anyone. My belief in God's goodness sustains me in stormy times."

Kelly spoke about his famous dancing sequence in *Singing in the Rain*, in which the character he plays splashes and dances spryly through the streets in a heavy rainstorm. "That sequence," he said, "was meant to be a regression to childhood: The character is so in love that he does everything like a child. The dancing in that number is really not that difficult. It's not a great dance as such. It's the *joie de vivre* of the number that makes it succeed."

Kelly likes being identified with that sequence, he confided, "because it represents what I've always tried to do. I think dancing in pictures should bring joy. It should be uplifting, rather than a medium for sending a message."

Kelly, it strikes me, found in dancing something akin to the "sacredness" that Martin Sheen found in acting. For Kelly's dancing comes across as a celebration of life—as a joyful expression of the life energy or light that the Creator has placed inside us. As Kelly put it, "What I've always tried to do with dancing is to bring joy."

The model. Actress and fashion model Brooke Shields is another entertainer who, more recently (1993), was willing to speak about her inner life and the peace she finds in prayer. "My life is so volatile," she said, "in the sense that I'm always traveling. I'm always moving around. People come in and out of my life.... Everything points to inconsistency. You go to do a movie for three months...and it's very intense, and then it's all over.

"The only thread that remains constant is faith—and Sunday Mass. That has been about the only thing consistent in my life. And I cling to that. I find there the one relationship that is unconditional and I sense there the unconditional forgiveness and love of God.

"I feel freer of judgment in Church.... I feel constantly judged in my life—whether by the press or the public or others. In a world where you are faced with judgment all the time, there is a sense of real freedom in knowing that there is one place where you can go and just *be*—and just think and be thankful.... It's the one place I can go and feel good about myself regularly."

Yet, says Shields, her relation to God is more than "popping into Church on Sunday for forty-five minutes. No, Sunday Eucharist is really a symbol and reminder of the way you try to live your life all the time."

———

PRAYER FOR CARRIERS OF LIGHT

God of Light,
we thank you for all those who reveal to us
the light, faith, sacredness and joy
that lies within them.

In so doing they offer us
an approachable image of you
who dwell in "inapproachable light."

May our light,
which is a sharing of your light,
not hide under a bushel,
but shine forth for others. Amen.

Lights Upon Dark Waters

A VERY DIFFERENT WRITING CHALLENGE faced me in 1982—an encounter with both profound darkness and astonishing light. I was part of a small team of journalists who had received grants to visit Hiroshima and Nagasaki to interview survivors of the 1945 atomic bombing of those two Japanese cities.

The 1945 atomic bombings represent one of the most harrowing human experiences of the twentieth century. This is true not only because of the tragic magnitude of those two bombings, whose combined explosions instantaneously killed at least one hundred seventy thousand people, but also because these bombs represented a new kind of weapon. The explosions of these two bombs blew open the doorway to a nuclear arms race that could potentially trigger an ultimate holocaust.

My purpose in this chapter is not to ascribe guilt or innocence to this or that nation. Rather, it is to explore the human potential for both darkness and light in all of us. A special darkness has always been linked with human hatred and war. Long before the nuclear age, the British poet Matthew Arnold described the field of battle as "a darkling plain on which ignorant armies clash by the night."

I can still remember the trepidation I felt as our bullet train from Tokyo approached Hiroshima. The train's throbbing and pounding motion seemed to invade my soul and trigger a profound anxiety. I grew tense as I looked out over the hazy rooftops of the city known by the whole world as the place where the first A-bomb fell. I had the uneasy premonition that I was about to peer into humanity's awesome capacity to destroy itself.

The day of the bombing. Indeed, the images remembered by the survivors were truly horrific. Ironically, a great flash of light accompanied those first nuclear blasts that caused so much human devastation. In Hiroshima the atomic bomb exploded eighteen hundred feet above the center of the city. A massive fireball was formed, ten times brighter than the sun, sending out heat so intense that it melted roof tiles directly below it. People exposed directly to the heat rays within a half-mile of the explosion had no chance whatsoever and died instantly from severe burns.

Many others died or were injured from the sudden explosive impact itself and from the glass and debris it sent flying through the air. Still others would die in the weeks ahead from the harmful doses of radiation they had received and which would, even years later, cause leukemia and other diseases.

It was not easy for us American and British journalists to listen day after day to the remembered images of the

A-bomb survivors:

- A group of young schoolgirls with torn clothes and charred bodies running around and frantically crying out "Mommy."

- Thousands of blackened corpses floating down the rivers.

- Bodies soaked with kerosene and cremated along the riverbanks or in schoolyards, often by family members of the dead.

What amazed me about the survivors with whom we talked was their spirit of peace. Many still bore scars suffered in the blast. A good number, for example, had ears missing, burnt off by the heat. As a rule, the people with whom we spoke were surprisingly not angry about their fate. Somehow, they had passed through a hell of human suffering and been transformed into gentle, peace-loving people. They commonly expressed the desire to work for peace among all nations. And they told their stories not to make listeners feel guilty, but so that the human family might avert similar disasters in the future.

It struck me that a parallel symbol of this kind of transformation was the Hiroshima Peace Park itself. The Peace Park, which sits directly under the explosion point of the world's first A-bomb, was once a smoldering desert. But now it has been transformed into an island of peace near Hiroshima's rebuilt city center. Dozens of monuments to the A-bomb victims are scattered about its grassy, tree-adorned lawns. Citizens from Japan and many other nations come by the thousands to visit the park week after week.

Compassion born of suffering. Akiro Takahashi is a good example of a survivor of the Hiroshima bombing whose suffering had ultimately not led him into bitterness but into a search for peace and understanding. When we spoke with him in 1982, he was director of the Hiroshima Peace Park Museum.

Takahashi told us that he was a schoolboy in 1945. On the day of the bombing, he was standing in a schoolyard less than a mile away from the blast. Parts of his head, back and arms were severely burned by the searing explosion. He lost both ears to burns. Shattered glass from the school windows flew into his elbow and hands, leaving his right hand disabled to this day.

We asked him questions in a lounge of the museum. He conveyed a spirit of compassion and serenity without any visible traces of anger or hatred toward those who dropped the bomb. How is it, I asked him, that he and so many of the other survivors seem to be so peaceful and to bear no anger about what has happened to them?

"There have been times," he replied, "when the other survivors and I felt anger toward the leaders of the Japanese government and military, as well as toward the leaders of the United States who made the decision to drop the bomb. We can't hide these feelings entirely or say we don't have them. But we must transcend them. Hatred on our side cannot erase hatred on the other side. We must overcome our grudges and hatred and work for understanding and peace between nations and races.

"Yes, we survivors have to overcome our grudges about the atomic bombing, and hope in turn that the Americans can overcome their grudges about Pearl Harbor. But I'm not saying that either side should forget the past. For it is in remembering the past that we may learn not to repeat it."

A similar attitude was expressed by Shigenobu Koji, a Buddhist monk who spoke with me in Hiroshima. He had family members killed or injured by the bomb. His father's temple was also demolished. He insisted that all human beings must recognize their human weakness and capacity for darkness and evil. "We have to transcend the discussion of who started the war or who committed the greatest atrocities," he said. "We must simply be conscious, on both sides, that we are capable of committing sin." Only then can we move toward peace and reconciliation, he added.

Tapping the light. My experience in Hiroshima and Nagasaki convinced me that there are immense dark forces in ourselves and in our world leading to fear, greed, hatred, distrust, vengeance, violence, war and unthinkable destruction. At the same time there are great capacities for light—for forgiveness and compassion and building a world of peace. We are capable either of tapping the light or succumbing to the darkness.

I saw amazing examples of tapping the light in those A-bomb survivors who were able to turn the ashes and rubble of their destroyed cities into peace parks and transform their tortured hearts into a loving search for global peace and harmony.

Another delicate sign of the victory of light over darkness was the paper-lantern ceremony the people of Hiroshima carry out each August 6 when they commemorate the bombing. On this date thousands of visitors stream into the Peace Park to honor and pray for their dead before the various shrines, quite conscious of the fiery horrors of 1945. When night falls, relatives of the victims come to the rivers next to the Peace Park with orange and yellow lanterns made of paper on a wood base. They set the candle-illuminated lanterns adrift on the dark waters as a way of offering consolation to the souls of the deceased, many of whom had floated on the same rivers in 1945.

The scene is one of quiet sadness. Yet the tranquility and beauty of thousands of glowing lanterns drifting soundlessly on the dark rivers as far as the eye can see is mysteriously consoling. To me, these lights are signals of hope and of God's goodness at work in the world. Despite the enormous damage and loss suffered amid the fire and violence and fury of war, the lanterns affirm that human dignity and beauty can prevail.

PRAYER FOR LIGHT IN TIMES OF DARKNESS

Gracious God, Fountain of Light,
help us embrace the good news
that behind the jagged mask of reality—
even behind the ignorance
and the dark capacities of the human heart—
we can still find a basis
for hope and peace and goodwill.

In short, we can find you,
our inextinguishable source of light. Amen.

The Real Meaning
of God's Light

W HEN WE TALK about God's light at work in the
world, we are not talking simply about physical
light. We are not talking primarily about sunlight or
starlight or the glow of lanterns or the light in a friend's
eyes. These are all symbols, metaphors and expressions—
and lovely expressions at that—of a richer and deeper
reality, namely, of the healing love of God at work in the
world.

Behind all these lights is really God's healing love. We
could say it in many other ways: We could say it is grace.
We could say it is God's saving presence and action in the
world and in our hearts. We could say it is God's goodness
and kindness. We could say it is God's reign among us—or
God's saving will or plan or word at work in human
history. However we express it, this light or healing love of
God is something we ultimately see by faith, not by sight.

Jesus brings light. Even a blind person can recognize this kind of light, while people who have the gift of sight may, ironically, be utterly blind to it. In John's Gospel, for example, we have the case of the blind man who clearly sees and accepts Jesus as the Light of the world while the Pharisees—who claim to be the enlightened, all-seeing teachers of the Law—do not recognize this Light (see John 9:1-41). The only thing the Pharisees see is that Jesus broke the law by giving the blind man sight on the sabbath. They refuse to recognize that the man who has just done God's healing work through a miraculous sign may have come from God.

And so it is the man born blind who points out the amazing blindness of those who consider themselves the brightest of teachers. "Never since the world began," the blind man informs the Pharisees, "has it been heard that anyone opened the eyes of a person born blind. If this man were not from God, he could do nothing" (John 9:32-33).

The Pharisees' response is to revile the man born blind and cast him out of their sight like a piece of dirt. On hearing the whole story a little later, Jesus reveals his identity more fully to the blind man and says: "I came into this world for judgment so that those who do not see may see, and those who do see may become blind" (John 9:39).

Jesus' obvious message is that people of humble faith— those who are open and ready to believe that God is at work in the world and within their hearts—will receive more light and healing. Those, however, who claim to know it all and close themselves to new signs of light will continue walking in darkness and sinful pride.

John's Gospel is also teaching us that the real meaning

of *light* is the healing work of God. Keep this in mind as you read what Jesus, encountering the blind man, says: "We have to do the works of him who sent me while it is day. Night is coming when no one can work. While I am in the world, I am the light of the world" (John 9:4-5, *New American Bible*).

As if to translate what being the "light of the world" means, John immediately describes Jesus performing a healing action: "When he had said this, he spat on the ground and made clay with the saliva, smeared the clay on his eyes, saying to him, 'Go wash in the Pool of Siloam....' So he went and washed and came back able to see" (John 9:6-7, *New American Bible*).

A mission of healing love. Jesus' use of clay in healing suggests Genesis 2:7 (*New American Bible*)—"God formed man from the clay of the ground...." The work of God in this world is to continue the work of creation. It is the work of bringing light, healing and fullness of life to humanity. Clearly, this was the work of Jesus. And just as clearly, it is to be the work of the followers of Jesus.

Jesus' work of healing love was certainly entrusted to the Church from the beginning. Throughout the centuries and continuing into the present, true followers of God's plan serve the sick, the blind, the lame and the oppressed. The Church has built hospitals and clinics to alleviate suffering in order to bring humanity to wholeness and peace.

This healing work of Jesus and of his Church makes clear what God's will is toward humanity. God's will is not that people suffer from disease and war and oppression, but just the opposite: that they be set free of these evils.

If we follow the Light of the World through the pages of the Gospels, we soon discover that we are following a trail of discarded stretchers, crutches, bandages and bonds of every kind. What better clues do we have of God's wishes and plan for the human family: namely, that it be healed and set free in every way?

PRAYER TO ACCEPT OUR ROLE IN HEALING

God, you send us healing love in Jesus.

Like him, we embrace our mission
to be the light of the world
while it is still day.

Nourished by your love,
we go out to do your work.

Make us instruments
of your light and healing and peace
in the world. Amen.

A Prophet's Light

DURING THE LAST twelve years of my life, I have pursued journalistic projects in at least a dozen Latin American countries, studying Spanish on the side. Ever since living in the Philippines I have been attracted to cultures shaped by a blend of native and Spanish influences.

On a more urgent level, I feel drawn to stories in these settings because the neediest people of our hemisphere are found there. These men, women and children are not neediest in terms of faith or cultural values or human dignity, but in terms of material poverty and political oppression. Like the blind man in the Gospel, they seek supporting hands as they try to lift themselves out of the darkness and into the light.

To me, one of the greatest principles of social justice is that the gifts of creation and resources of the planet are intended by the Creator for the enjoyment of all. All human beings have an equal right to sit at the table of creation. In many developing countries, however, including those of Latin America, wealth and resources and power are controlled by a handful of wealthy families or private groups. We see a parallel on a global level, where the rich industrialized nations of the North tend to control and gobble up a disproportionate percentage of the world's resources.

The great majority of people in many countries—and this often includes the native peoples of these lands—have little access to power, wealth, education, health care and other opportunities that would allow them to gain a fairer share of the earth's blessings. A strong military and police force are often installed in these countries to protect the interests of the wealthy. In effect, if not always by intention, this keeps the poor in their place.

Occasionally, courageous defenders of the poor rise up. Like true prophets, they proclaim the Good News of God's Kingdom and urge the transformation of human society. They call for the change of social and legal structures so that all men and women can better realize their full dignity and rights—and a fairer share of the gifts of creation.

The light of Archbishop Oscar Romero. One such prophet and defender of the poor was Oscar Romero, archbishop of San Salvador, the capital of El Salvador. He became an eloquent voice for those without a voice and was killed in 1980 by an assassin's bullet while he was celebrating Mass.

In 1984 I went to that Central American country to gather material for a story about the archbishop. Perhaps an article about the man could help bring his message to a larger audience. I was able to visit Romero's tomb and the hospital chapel where he was murdered and other places important to his memory. I talked with people who had worked closely with him. They left me with no doubt that he was a courageous and holy shepherd who laid down his life for the sheep.

Archbishop Romero, I was told, represents a new model of Church leadership that has been arising in the second half of the twentieth century. Those who champion his cause hope that an increasing number of Church leaders will take his lead and move away from aligning themselves primarily with the rich and powerful. They hope, instead, that the leaders of tomorrow will opt for solidarity with the poor, as Romero himself did.

Archbishop Romero's own words give an inkling of his great compassion for the poor and the kind of light and prophetic courage that shone forth from him:

> The Church is persecuted because it wants to be truly the Church of Christ. As long as the Church preaches an eternal salvation without involving itself in the real problems of the world, the Church is respected and praised and is even given privileges. But if it is faithful to its mission of denouncing the sin that puts many in misery, and if it proclaims the hope of a more just and human world, then it is persecuted and slandered and called subversive and Communist (*Faith, the Church and Political Commitment*, pastoral letter released August 6, 1977).

In a homily given exactly one month before his assassination, the archbishop pleaded for conversion and the end of violence from those higher-ups who controlled the country's wealth and power:

Let them share what they are and have. Let them not keep silencing with violence the voice of those of us who offer this invitation. Let them not keep killing those of us who are trying to achieve a more just sharing of the power and wealth of our country. I speak in the first person, because this week I received notice that I am on the list of those who are to be eliminated.... But let it be known that no one can kill the voice of justice.

In one sense, a bright light of hope was snuffed out when Archbishop Romero was assassinated. In a deeper sense, however, his light has never gone out. Indeed, Romero's renown continues to grow, and he has passed on to the Church a fresh and much needed light—the blazing torch of a new style of leadership.

———————

PRAYER FOR PROPHETIC LIGHT

Loving Creator,
may we absorb your light
as it shines forth from courageous leaders
who stand with the oppressed.

Help us to see the poor
with your caring eyes.

Give us the wisdom, creativity and charity
to bring about a fairer distribution

of the earth's bounty
so that one day all people
may enjoy your blessings. Amen.

Light for Those
Sitting in Darkness

HISTORY BOOKS ARE usually written from the viewpoint of those in power. The people on top—the so-called "movers and shakers"—often control the version of truth that appears in our textbooks, not to mention our newspapers.

The Archbishop Romeros of the world, by contrast, assume the perspective of the poor and the powerless rather than that of the rich and powerful. This is not an entirely new way of looking at things. The same viewpoint is taken by Jesus in the Gospels and by the prophets of many religious traditions.

I wish I could claim that the poor's point of view has always been my own. Being white, male and North American, however, often makes it very difficult for me (and others like me) to see things totally from the perspective of those stripped of all power or advantage. Yet, in my heart of hearts, I certainly want to come closer to this perspective.

Of tear gas and water cannons. There have been times in Latin America when this perspective has been thrust upon me. These encounters have given me at least some inkling of how people with little or no power see things, especially as they face the immense machinery of oppression.

In 1987, for example, while General Augusto Pinochet still held dictatorial sway in Chile, I got a taste, literally, of how oppressive regimes use various forms of intimidation, including tear gas and water cannons, to squelch efforts for justice on behalf of abused and oppressed people.

I was with three other religious journalists on a five-day fact-gathering trip to Santiago, Chile, under the auspices of the Washington Office on Latin America, a U.S. organization which monitors human rights practices. Among the people we interviewed were widows whose husbands or other family members had been murdered, detained by security forces or disappeared. The widows belonged to the Association of Families of the Detained and Disappeared. By peaceful demonstrations in front of the presidential palace, this group was trying to pressure the government to bring these cases to justice. They wanted to put an end to the nightmare of murder, torture, violence and oppression that was rampant in their country.

One morning our group of journalists went to observe a special commemoration planned by three of the widows in front of the presidential palace. It was the second anniversary of their husbands' deaths. The peaceful commemoration was barely underway when the police with their armored vehicles and water cannons began dispersing the crowds. The three other journalists and I arrived at the scene only to see the protest already being crushed by the police. We could still see their vehicles going up and down the streets, dousing the crowds with water cannons.

Little pockets of protesters, however, were still demonstrating on some of the back streets. A young Chilean woman, a Church worker, grabbed my sleeve and led me to a place a few blocks away where demonstrators were reassembling. A group of young people, some with photos of the murder victims, were shouting at uniformed police, singing protest songs and calling for justice.

Suddenly the armored water trucks began moving into this district, shooting streams of water at the demonstrators. Smaller police vehicles also began rushing in from many sides, and soldiers began throwing tear gas canisters. These were exploding at the feet of the demonstrators, who were fleeing from spreading clouds of gas. With eyes burning, my companion and I, like many others, were ducking into alleyways and shops trying to escape the tear gas, the jets of water and possible arrest. There were moments when I was gripped with terror at the thought of the police spotting my camera and confiscating it. Much more frightening was the thought of the police dragging my companion and me away into their vehicles—perhaps to join the vast ranks of "the disappeared."

This experience helped me understand, rather concretely, the perspective of oppressed people struggling for political change. The opportunity to stand—and run!—in their shoes, if only for a brief moment, was for me one of those special moments of illumination encountered on life's path. I suddenly saw and felt—from the inside—the vulnerability of those struggling for justice in the face of military regimes and governments with powerful mechanisms of control and intimidation at their disposal.

I could also imagine, in addition, the encouragement these groups must feel when they see other committed people stand in solidarity with them. How important it must be to them, for example, when they see an immense and powerful institution like the Church courageously taking up their cause. Let me explain with an example.

Signs of solidarity. Just a few days after I returned to the United States after my five-day stay in Chile, Pope John Paul II visited that country. I watched the news reports very closely and read all that I could to see what the pope would say or do during his visit to Chile. Would the pope and the Chilean Church, for example, show any clear signs of siding with the poor and the oppressed?

Some Chileans feared that Pinochet would manipulate the papal visit so as to strengthen his own repressive stance against human rights groups. The opposite seemed to happen. Though the pope's purpose in coming to Chile was to make a pastoral visit—not precisely to tackle social and political issues—he did nevertheless speak out more than once against oppression and human rights violations. Not unlike Archbishop Romero, the pope defended the Church's task of siding with the poor and advocating a more just society.

Pinochet and his government had often denounced the

Church for its support of human rights. In fact, they repeatedly told the Church to stick to prayer and the sacraments and stay out of politics and social reform. The pope argued against this viewpoint as he talked with reporters during his flight to Chile. He told the reporters that those are wrong who say, "Stay in the sacristy and do nothing else!" Describing the Pinochet regime as "dictatorial," the pope said the Chilean Church should defend human rights and encourage the transition to democracy.

When the pope preached to the Chilean bishops two days later, he told them: "Never hesitate to defend always, before all, the legitimate rights of the person, created in the image and likeness of God. Proclaim your preferential love for the poor...."

In Punta Arenas, the pope told the crowds that the Church "denounces the practices of physical and moral torture.... Let us pledge ourselves to overcoming injustices, to respecting the legitimate rights of the human being, to a better and fairer distribution of wealth..., which will improve the lives of so many Chileans...."

The pope's strongest statement against oppression was not expressed in words but in a symbolic encounter that denounced the violence of the Pinochet regime more effectively than any words could achieve. I refer to the pope's meeting with Carmen Gloria Quintana, one of two young women violently attacked by the military while demonstrating during a general strike just nine months before the papal visit. The women were beaten, drenched with gasoline and set on fire. The other woman died.

Quintana survived third-degree burns on fifty percent of her body.

The pope had specifically asked to meet with Quintana, knowing full well that she was an international symbol of Chilean repression and a living reproach to the violent extremes of the Pinochet dictatorship. Before TV cameras, the pope put his hands on her scarred face and embraced her three times. "I am the youth burned by the military," she told the pope. "I know," he answered. "I understand everything. You have suffered much. I bless you in the name of God."

I do not mean to imply by showcasing this powerful gesture of solidarity that popes or other Church leaders have always been exemplary in running to the support of the oppressed—or that the Church's record is blameless in this regard. (The Church has certainly made its share of mistakes!) In the case just described, however, the pope was placing himself, as well as the Church, in dramatic solidarity with all those who suffer violence at the hands of the powerful. As such, this public demonstration of the Church's willingness to stand with the victims of oppression deserves to be praised and set forth as a model for the future.

The millions of poor people watching this encounter on television must have felt immensely affirmed by it. Indeed, for all those sitting in darkness and the shadow of death, such compassionate gestures seem like the morning sun coming over the horizon and beaming light upon the world.

PRAYER TO SEE WITH THE POOR

Incarnate Word,
your viewpoint was always that of the poor.

In fact, you were poor.

You did not chose a palace for your birthplace,
or affluent parents,
but a simple stable
and a humble mother and father.

Your identifying with needy people
offers a great light of hope for us all—
and an example to be followed.

Stay with us always. Amen.

Fiery Seraph Wings

I N THE SUMMER OF 1988 I fulfilled a lifelong
yearning to visit Mount La Verna in Italy, where Francis
of Assisi underwent the climactic mystical experience of
his life—a moment of ecstatic union with his crucified
Savior. The encounter left Francis branded on his hands,
feet and side with the stigmata, the five wounds of Christ.

La Verna is the holy mountain of the Franciscan
tradition. This wild and secluded height was given to
Francis and his companions as a place for solitary prayer
by a certain Count Orlando who had been inspired by
Francis' preaching in 1213. Over the centuries, many
followers of Francis have sought to visit this place of holy
retreat sometime before their death. And so it was with me
that summer of '88, in which I was marking my twenty-
fifth anniversary as a Franciscan priest.

Traveling by myself on a bus that was twisting along a
mountain road, I remember looking out of the window,
still some twenty miles from La Verna. I had no clear idea
of what to look for at that distance, but suddenly on the
horizon I saw a rugged mountain that I knew in my soul

had to be Mount La Verna. Jutting upward from the mountain was a large outcropping of rock that, to my eye, resembled a shark's fin. That mountain, I thought, could certainly appeal to something valiant and mystical and fierce in the heart of Francis.

When I arrived there, I was surprised at the complex of buildings spread out and half-hidden on its rocky precipices—a large friary, a basilica and various chapels, lodging space and dining rooms for the many pilgrims and followers of Saint Francis who come to make retreats in this out-of-the-way place. Staying here a day and a night with the friars, I thought, would give me a chance to ponder the amazing event that took place on these rocky heights near the end of Francis' life.

An account of Francis' vision. The Chapel of the Stigmata is perched on the edge of the same sheer precipice where Saint Francis stood two years before his death and where he was swept up into the mystery of God's overwhelming love for him and for humanity.

Saint Bonaventure, in his *Life of St. Francis*, describes Francis as being more inflamed than usual with the love of God as he began a special time of solitary prayer at La Verna that September of 1224. "His unquenchable fire of love for the good Jesus," Bonaventure writes, "was fanned into such a blaze of flames that many waters could not quench so powerful a love" (see Song of Solomon 8:6-7).

Bonaventure goes on: "While Francis was praying on the mountainside, he saw a Seraph with six fiery and shining wings descend from the height of heaven. And when in swift flight the Seraph had reached a spot in the air near the man of God, there appeared between the wings the figure of a man crucified, with his hands and feet extended in the form of a cross and fastened to a cross. Two of the wings were lifted above his head, two were extended for flight and two covered his whole body.

"When Francis saw this, he was overwhelmed and his heart was flooded with a mixture of joy and sorrow. He rejoiced because of the gracious way Christ looked upon him under the appearance of a Seraph, but the fact that he was fastened to a cross *pierced his soul with a sword* of compassionate sorrow (Luke 2:35)."

When the vision disappeared, writes Bonaventure, Francis was left with a "marvelous ardor" in his heart. At the same time, there were "imprinted on his body markings that were no less marvelous." These markings were the stigmata.

There are two things to dwell on here. First is the Seraph. Seraphs are those angels closest to God, burning with love as they bow before the most high God, shouting "Holy, holy, holy!" Their fiery wings, as depicted here, suggest the flaming intensity of God's love that Christ communicated to Francis, which in turn, set Francis' heart afire. The word *seraphic* is often used to describe Francis' passionate style of relating to God and is often applied to the whole Franciscan Order, which is sometimes called the Seraphic Order.

Second, we focus on "the gracious way Christ looked upon him." This is something of a repeat of the vision Francis had in the beginning of his spiritual life in which

"Jesus appeared to him fastened on a cross" and "Francis' soul melted at the sight, and the memory of Christ's passion was so impressed on the innermost recesses of his heart that from that hour whenever Christ's crucifixion came to mind, he could scarcely contain his tears and sighs..." (Bonaventure's *Life of St. Francis*).

The God who gives all. Here at La Verna, Francis was set aflame all the more by the experience of the unimaginable love of God, who holds nothing back, not even the life of God's only Son. For Francis, to look at the intensity of Jesus' love beaming toward him from the cross was like looking into the sun. It was blinding—overwhelming.

Francis had seen this same kind of soul-blinding love revealed in the Incarnation—in the Word's becoming flesh in Bethlehem in the form of a vulnerable, naked baby. He saw the same brilliance in that awesome central gesture of the Last Supper and of every Eucharist: Jesus handing over his Body and Blood—his complete self—to those he loved.

This experience of God's total self-emptying explains Francis' love for poverty. If the God-man could be poor—not clutching anything of his own, not even the divine nature, but accepting the poverty and nakedness of a crude manger at Bethlehem and the cross at Calvary—then Francis too could respond with self-giving and hold nothing back in his love of Christ.

Saint Anthony of Padua, an early follower of Francis, once proclaimed in a sermon words that seem to be inspired by Francis' own style of loving: "Love wholly and not partially," Anthony encouraged the crowds. "God does not have parts but is present totally everywhere." In the same way, Anthony adds, "God does not want only a part of you.... Give all of yourself and God will give you all of himself."

This is a good description of the real meaning of poverty as taught by Saint Francis. For Francis, poverty was not a matter of pinching pennies or scolding his friars for touching coins. That was not the point at all. His horror was at the specter of a stingy spirit. His poverty was a willingness to give away the whole store—always to pour out generously all that he had, thus imitating the unbounded goodness of God, who is never grasping and greedy about anything. Francis' poverty was a readiness to hand everything over to God and neighbor. Francis' receiving the stigmata at La Verna was a confirmation that the holy man during his life had mirrored the "poverty" of God. For Francis now bore in his own flesh the five signs of God's total self-giving—the pierced hands, feet and side.

For Franciscans, the self-sacrificing love of Jesus, as revealed in the cross, is the shining summit of God's revelation. The richest revelation of God's word and goodness peaks in Jesus, especially in his self-emptying death and resurrection. "No one has greater love than this, to lay down one's life for one's friends" (John 15:13). This is why the cross has been central for Franciscans and, of course, for Christianity itself.

Every day, all around the world, because Francis requested the practice, Franciscans pray the *Adoramus te*: "We adore you, O Lord, here and in all the churches throughout the whole world, and we bless you because by your holy cross you have redeemed the world." Their coat of arms, moreover, is a cross with two arms crossing and nailed to it. One arm is that of Francis; the other is Christ's. Both arms reveal a willingness to give all!

PRAYER FOR A SERAPHIC HEART

God of love, lead us
to the wild, solitary spot in our own hearts
where we may encounter your gift of fiery love
and see the gracious way
you look upon us from the cross.

Help us to open ourselves
to your limitless love,
which holds nothing back from us.

May our hearts catch some of the seraphic flame
that marked Francis' all-out response
to your great love. Amen.

Letting God Love Us

I N THE LAST HALF of my life, a gradual illumination
has affected my understanding of God's will. This
intuition or insight has made my soul feel lighter and
brighter—more joyful.

In my younger years, God's will was something dark
and gloomy for me. I identified it as a whole system of laws
and commandments I was obligated to follow if I wanted
to please God and gain salvation. In those years, when I
prayed, "Thy will be done," in the Our Father, I thought of
it mainly in terms of *my* responsibility—and often a
gloomy one at that—to obey a set of rules so God would
love me.

Today when I think of God's will, it is something very
different. Now the idea nearly glows with light. I think of
it, first of all, as God's loving plan to lead me and all God's
people to healing and happiness. I see God's will today
more as Francis saw it, namely, as God's desire to love us
unconditionally and to lead us to abundance of life. "God's
glory," as Saint Irenaeus put it, "is the human being fully
alive."

Now when I pray, "Thy will be done," it has a more joyful ring because God's will or plan is to bring total healing and life to all those whom God loves. One can only respond gratefully and lovingly to such a wonderful plan!

God's will prompts a joyful response. I still see, of course, a clear link between God's will and God's commandments, but these commandments take on their true meaning only *after* I understand God's overarching and loving will that I be happy and fully alive. Obeying God's will is not, first of all, a dreary task of following lots of rules and piling up good deeds so that God will think well of me. God already loves me immeasurably and wishes to save me.

My obeying, my moral task, therefore, is not a matter of bringing God's love into existence (God's love is already there!), but rather one of *responding* to that love. And I respond to it by joyfully, gratefully and affectionately trying to follow God's commandments. For they are now seen not as cold disciplinary rules to burden my spirit, but as loving guidelines for discovering fullness of life.

Obeying God's will calls for "response-ability" rather than responsibility. Leading a good moral life is not the cause of God's loving and saving me, but its consequence. God's gift of love comes before my task of responding to it, and not the other way around.

Don't leave God out of the equation. God desperately wants to be in a growing love union with us. There are two sides to such a love relationship: God's side and ours. Too often we overlook God's side of it and focus mainly on our side of the relationship, our responsibility: We have to work harder to purge our guilt, show more discipline, flex more muscle, grit more teeth, multiply our prayers and acts of penance—and then union with God will be better.

Yes, these efforts are important and Jesus himself urged us to love God "with all our strength." But I can see God smiling at us as we work so frantically. Finally, God asks us: "Hey, remember me? I'm a part of this equation too! Lighten up a little. I see you trying so hard to make yourself into something important. Is what you and I have a love relationship—or a one-man show?

"Relax. Just let my love enter your heart. I've already created you in my image. You are already important. You already have everything. I've laid down my life for you, held nothing back from you, forgiven your guilt. I appreciate your show of goodwill. But I wouldn't mind it if you gave me a little more attention—or told me you need me! Open your heart more to me and let me give more of myself to you. Then our love union can really start to sing!"

I believe this is what Jesus was trying to convey to us by his famous parable about the Pharisee and the tax collector. He shows the Pharisee sashaying to the front of the temple to tell God about the big stack of virtues he has piled up—his fasting, his paying tithes on all his income. It is a prayer of self-congratulation.

Meanwhile the tax collector barely dares to raise his eyes. He strikes his breast and prays, "O God, be merciful to me, a sinner." It is this humble man who recognizes which side of his relationship with God carries the most vitality and importance. It is not his power that is so important but God's. The most needed attitude on his part is a humble openness and responsiveness to God's great goodness and mercy!

Affection is the Franciscan way. This brings us back to Francis and his La Verna experience. Although Francis had performed great acts of bodily penance during his life (which he later regretted as abuse of "Brother Body"), he nevertheless focused on the great outpouring of love coming from God's side of the relationship. And Francis left himself open so that the love of his crucified Lover could come flowing in and ignite a response of great affection within him.

Saint Bonaventure wrote a book called *The Soul's Journey Into God*, in which he presents Francis' La Verna model of prayer as the surest way to reach a more intimate union with God. (Bonaventure was a Franciscan friar who, just twenty years after Francis' death, had become a bright light at the University of Paris, both as a student and as a teacher of theology. Down the road, he would also become the head of the Franciscan Order and a cardinal of the Catholic Church.) In *The Soul's Journey Into God*, Bonaventure takes his cue from the unlettered Francis rather than from all the wonderful things he had learned at the university. Deepening one's union with God, he had discovered, is more a matter of the heart and of affection than of keen intellect.

Bonaventure wrote his book while he was Minister General of the Order and while making a retreat at La Verna some thirty-three years after the death of Saint

Francis. In the prologue he calls to mind "the miracle which had occurred to blessed Francis in this very place: the vision of a winged Seraph in the form of the Crucified." For Bonaventure, an ardent union with the Crucified, like that experienced by Francis, is the surest road into the fire of God's love.

"There is no other path," writes Bonaventure, "but through the burning love of the Crucified, a love which so transformed Saint Paul into Christ when he was carried up to the Third Heaven (2 Corinthians 12:2) that he could say: With Christ I am nailed to the Cross. I live, now not I, but Christ lives in me (Galatians 2:20). This love also so absorbed the soul of Francis that his Spirit shone through his flesh when two years before his death he carried in his body the sacred stigmata of the passion."

Bonaventure stresses that Francis' style of prayer is marked by "unction" and "devotion" rather than scholarly speculation. "Affection" is more important than "erudition of the intellect."

Near the end of his book, Bonaventure sums up everything in the following list of preferences that those seeking union with God should ask for in prayer: "Ask grace not instruction, desire not understanding, the groaning of prayer not diligent reading, the Spouse not the teacher, God not man, darkness not clarity, not light but the fire that totally inflames and carries us into God by ecstatic unctions and burning affections. This fire is God, and *his furnace is in Jerusalem* [Isaiah 31:9]; and Christ enkindles it in the heat of his burning passion...."

PRAYER TO THE SPOUSE

God of love,
I come to you as to a Spouse
rather than to a teacher.

Your own love burns so much stronger than my own
that it scares me.

Yet I open myself
to your beauty and transforming fire.

Help set my own heart aflame
so we can reach a deeper union still—
and even happier days
working as partners in the Kingdom. Amen.

A Dozen Red Roses

I N THE SUMMER OF 1993 I was visiting the Franciscan Church of St. Peter in the Chicago Loop. The popular church stands on West Madison Street in the middle of the financial district and is dwarfed by surrounding skyscrapers. Thousands of people visit the church each week—businesspeople with briefcases, street people, shoppers, tourists and passersby.

As I rambled around the inside of the church, something made me stop at the large statue of the Sacred Heart of Jesus at one of the side aisles. There I was astonished to see, lying at the foot of the statue, a dozen fresh red roses. They were not arranged in a vase. Someone apparently had just come in off the street and laid them at the foot of the statue!

Who placed this lovely bouquet there? I wondered. A businessman? A streetwalker overcome with love for Christ? A rich widow? A lover with a broken heart whose intended companion had stood him up? A poor person who scraped up forty dollars to lay this extravagant token of love before the Savior? Whoever left it there, I decided, was a person with a temperament like Saint Francis'.

The dozen roses became, for me, a symbol of the seraphic ideal of seeking God with affection and emotion, not just intellectually. For Francis and his followers, the goal of religion is not so much to comprehend the God who is Truth as to fall in love with the God who is Goodness. If and when Franciscans go to heaven, they want more than the beatific vision of the God who represents eternal truth. They seek, even more, the beatific embrace of the God who is goodness and love!

'I want my friars to be minstrels!' For Saint Francis, the following of Christ is not seen as a burden on one's back but a song in one's heart. The saint always seemed to hear the music of God's love in his heart—and he responded with joy and affection and even a bit of flamboyant romance.

At times, according to Francis' biographer Thomas of Celano, Francis would be walking along and suddenly get carried away by the thought of God's goodness. The saint would pick up two sticks from the ground, tuck one under his chin like a violin and move the other over it like a bow. Then he would sing in French songs of love and praise to God. "This whole ecstasy of joy," Celano writes, "would often end in tears and his song of gladness would be dissolved in compassion for the passion of Christ" (*A Second Life of St. Francis*, #127).

Francis wanted music and song even when he was dying. He asked his brother friars to praise God with him by singing the *Canticle of the Creatures* which he had composed while he was ill and going blind. He used to say, moreover, that he wanted his friars to go about the world like minstrels to "inspire the hearts of people and stir them to spiritual joy."

Some followers of Francis are still trying to do this today. In the early 1990's in Cincinnati, I attended a farewell ceremony for one of our Franciscan friars, Silas Oleksinski, O.F.M., who at age sixty-eight had volunteered to serve in the former Soviet Union where, after the fall of Communism, new mission possibilities were opening up. I was moved by the courage and great faith of this friar, who, at an age when most people are settling into a life of retirement, was risking separation from loved ones and facing fears of the unknown.

In the true spirit of Franciscan exuberance, Silas did an amazing thing near the close of the ceremony, as the choir began singing "How Great Thou Art." It was one of those crazy, creative Franciscan moments that observers of the Order have almost come to expect. The friar walked up to the microphone and began whistling with the choir—with a loud and clear, marvelously warbling whistle—all the way to the last note! Many could not hold back tears because of this bold gesture of love and joyful faith. It was an almost literal compliance with Francis' wish that his followers go through the world like minstrels.

Prayer for an Affectionate Heart

Loving God,
we praise you and thank you
for your overflowing goodness.

Help us always to hear
the melody of your great love for us.

Give our hearts joy
that we may respond to your love
with singing and great affection.

And may we always come to you
with a dozen red roses in our hands. Amen.

Gifts From Clare

I T WAS AUGUST 11, 1993. I took lunch, as was my custom, at St. Francis Friary, our Franciscan headquarters across the street from the *St. Anthony Messenger* building. After lunch I stopped to say a prayer in the friary chapel. At the foot of the altar, I noticed a picture of Saint Francis and Saint Clare of Assisi standing together. It had been placed there, alongside some flowers, because it was the feast of Saint Clare. With the support of Saint Francis, Clare founded the order of Franciscan women who became known as the Poor Clares, or simply the Clares. August 11, 1993, was also the date on which the worldwide Franciscan family had chosen to celebrate the eight hundredth anniversary of Clare's birth.

The daughter of a noble Assisian family, Clare was known for her deep spirituality and love for the poor. Her heart was attracted to the radical gospel way of life preached by Francis. Secretly one night, to the dismay of her family, Clare met with Francis and his small band of brothers to commit her life to God and to begin a community of women devoted to living the gospel. Clare and the holy women who followed her and continue to follow her in our day have always been a revered and vital part of the Franciscan movement. The Clares serve as a vibrant model of contemplative prayer and the kind of intense loving union with God which all Franciscans, and indeed all human beings, are meant to seek.

A feast day favor. Clare, whose name means "light" or "bright," has indeed been a brilliant source of light for the Franciscan Order and the Church. At the time of my visit to the friary chapel, I had already chosen *Lights* as the title and theme of this book. As I sat there looking at the picture of Clare and Francis, I asked Clare a favor on the occasion of her feast. Would she share with me some light on prayer and contemplative union with God?

Almost immediately, the realization came to me that if our prayer lacks vitality at times, it is because we are not relating to God, but only to concepts of God. The best prayer is when we are dealing not with *ideas* about God but with the living God.

Suddenly, my awareness shifted. I left behind my ideas and images, as it were, and simply sat in the realness of God—the God of beauty, the God of far-flung galaxies and vast oceans, the God of all the nations of peoples of all centuries. During that "gifted moment" of prayer, the vastness and the goodness of God touched me, not just theological concepts of these mysteries. I felt high—and at one with the immediacy of God.

The experience helped me understand how Francis could spend whole nights in prayer, simply repeating "My

God and my all!" He was not analyzing concepts of God. He was embracing God, who is larger, lovelier and more mysterious than any word or concept—the God who "is not far from each one of us. For 'In him we live and move and have our being' " (Acts 17:27b-28). It made me recall, as well, that prayer can be as simple as a loving couple holding hands and sitting in silent admiration before a sunset. It's an experience—a relationship—not an exercise in thinking. There is no need for words or thoughts. The couple is content simply to rest quietly and lovingly in each other's presence.

Evaluating our prayer experiences, I know, is tricky. Prayer cannot be judged on the basis of "highs" or "feel good" experiences. All I can say is that for me my experience on Clare's feast was another of those lights that God gives each of us on our journeys. To this day I consider it a special gift from Clare.

'Desert experiences' have value too. The next day, I was sharing my experience with the small Poor Clare community in Cincinnati. I was most gently reminded by one of the Clares that although such highs are rightly to be savored, there are dangers in trying to rank our experiences of prayer. Who is to say that the dry periods and the "dark nights of the soul" that we all experience in prayer are less important moments than the so-called highs? These less savory experiences, she added, reveal our human frailty and darkness and finiteness. As such, these elements of self-knowledge are very useful in our love union with God. To experience our nakedness, our whole unvarnished reality, is not without value. "What a person is before God is who he or she is—and nothing more," according to Saint Francis.

This sensitively shared reminder was an additional blessing for me—the second gift I received from Clare in two days!

PRAYER TO EXPERIENCE THE LIVING GOD

My God and my all,
you are so much more vibrant
than our weak ideas of you.

Free us from the prison
of our narrow preconceptions and stereotypes
and let the real "us" embrace the real "you"
as you are.

Praise and honor and glory to you
forever and ever. Amen.

His Face Shining Like the Sun

A S I WRITE THESE final words, it is spring of 1995.
Fewer than five years remain before the year 2000,
which signals the beginning of the third millennium since
the birth of the Word made flesh.

That our world is wracked with problems is no secret.
Those wishing to tap into darkness rather than light can
certainly find instances of darkness around us: Violence
and guns and drugs multiply in our streets and even in our
homes. Bloody conflicts rage around the world. Terrorist
bombs kill and maim children and other innocent people.
Fascism and racism, among other "isms," rise like dark
clouds over our world. Abortion, child abuse, poverty,
disease, ecological blight, earthquake, flood and famine fill
us with dismay.

Not surprisingly, as a new millennium approaches,
self-appointed prophets are predicting with apocalyptic
fervor the end of the world and the collapse of civilization.
To me, such announcements of cosmic disintegration are
more a result of our psychological habit of projecting upon
the world our own inner insecurity, guilt feelings or fears

of retribution than of any real threat of sudden cataclysm. We can safely recognize as abnormal, I believe, the fears of doomsayers who gather in caves or concrete bunkers, proclaiming that the world will end on such and such a date. Such predictions, century after century, have proven to be unfounded, and are rightly ignored. Jesus himself says we "know neither the day nor the hour" (see Matthew 25:13).

On the other hand, our encounters with darkness, sin, social upheaval and even natural disasters are not without value. They can lead us to a healthy fear and respect for our true state: vulnerability. It is a state we share with all living creatures. And it is OK—indeed, illuminating—to feel vulnerable and insecure, to recognize our own mortality and the fragileness of our passing world.

God has good intentions toward us. The accent is best placed not upon our weakness and insecurity but upon God's goodness. For our Guardian never sleeps. God's light and care always go with us, even in times of darkness and loss. My basic affirmation is this: Behind the mask of reality lies neither a black void nor some sinister plot for our destruction but a God of incredible goodness and light.

For those of us in the Judeo-Christian tradition, the pages of Scripture are filled with multiple signs of God's overflowing goodness. Indeed, images of abundance keep jumping out at us from all sides. For example, Genesis 2:6, 10 presents a wondrous image of a stream welling up from the ground that soon becomes a river to water the garden and all its trees, including the tree of life in its middle.

Ezekiel 47 describes an immense flow of water bursting from the temple—fresh water that rises higher than the waist, then so high that the wading prophet can only cross this river by swimming. In this river of life, fish are abundant, and fishermen stand by with their nets to make large catches.

In the Gospels, too, we can hardly miss similar images of God's great bounty. We find there an echo of Ezekiel: The disciples' nets bulge and burst with large catches of fish (see, for example, Luke 5:1-6; John 21:4-6). Then, on the hillside, we see Jesus multiplying loaves and fishes to feed enormous crowds—with twelve baskets of fragments left over (Mark 5:35-44)! At the wedding in Cana, too, we watch with amazement as Jesus replenishes the dwindling wine supply by changing water into wine—not by the glass or bottle, but by giant earthen water jars! There are six, "each holding twenty or thirty gallons" (John 2:6). What a picture of divine bounty! What divine affirmation of marriage and human love! Surely, our cup runs over!

The abundant life of the risen Savior. The resurrection of Jesus is itself an expression of God's bountiful life. Life is not ended at death but enhanced. The resurrection stories bristle with new life, as surely as they radiate fresh light!

When Jesus breaks forth from the dark tomb and appears to his disciples, it's almost as if he has turned into light. Indeed, even the angel at the tomb who announces the news of Jesus' resurrection was a vision of light. "His appearance was like lightning and his clothing white as snow," according to Matthew 28:3. Jesus seems as light as air as he vanishes from people's sight or passes through walls—or amazes his disciples with the buoyant message: "Do not be afraid!" (see Matthew 28:10).

In the Book of Revelation John's vision of the risen Savior is shot through with light. Jesus radiates light as he stands among seven gold lampstands: "His head and his hair were white as white wool, white as snow; his eyes were like a flame of fire.... In his right hand he held seven stars,...and his face was like the sun shining with full force" (Revelation 1:14-16). Could this not be the lead actor of human history—his face now glowing with light—coming back for his final bow at the end of the drama of salvation? Whatever the case, John is stunned by the brilliance of this vision. "When I saw him," writes the seer, "I fell at his feet as though dead. But he placed his right hand on me, saying, 'Do not be afraid; I am the first and the last, and the living one. I was dead, and see, I am alive forever and ever;...'" (1:17-18).

Earlier, in the Gospels, a similar thing had happened. Jesus went up a high mountain with three disciples and was transfigured before them—radiating light: "[H]is face shone like the sun, and his clothes became dazzling white," writes Matthew. There, too, the disciples fell down as though dead—until Jesus touched them and used the same words: "Do not be afraid" (see Matthew 17:1-8).

In all these examples we see the divine light bursting through Jesus' humanity. His human nature becomes flooded with the light of God. The Word shines through the flesh as light through glass. As the Nicene Creed affirms, Jesus Christ, is "God from God, Light from

Light,...one in Being with the Father." When Jesus comes again, surely his face will be shining like the sun.

Embracing the light. Our mission—our destiny, too—is to let God's word shine through our humanity. We open our hearts to God's light. We let it soak in. And then, in loving response, we go out to convey that light to others.

Each year at the Easter Vigil, Christians engage in a ritual of light that models this process for us. There is a solemn lighting of the new fire and of the Easter Candle, representing the risen and glorified Christ, the Light of the world. The people take fire from that lampstand and pass its light to the candles of their neighbors until the whole assembly glows with light.

The challenge to embrace God's glorious light and goodness and pass it on to others is not my invention. Saint Paul encountered and passed on that same challenge almost two millennia ago. On the way to Damascus he met the risen Jesus amid a great flash of light. What Paul encountered was more than a concept or a new idea of God's love. It was a blinding experience of the love of God shining through the bright mirror of Jesus Christ. For the remainder of his life, Paul, the great evangelist, carried that experience of light and transmitted it, by preaching and by letter, to those sitting in darkness and distress.

Paul would write to the Christians being persecuted in Rome, for example, and tell them about a good God whose burning love holds nothing back and can never be extinguished. Paul's message, of course, was meant for all of us. For are not the anxieties and stresses of our age very much like those of Paul's? "If God is for us," Paul assures those suffering in Rome,

> who is against us? He who did not withhold his own Son, but gave him up for all of us, will he not with him also give us everything else?...Who will separate us from the love of Christ? Will hardship, or distress, or persecution, or famine, or nakedness, or peril, or sword?... No, in all these things we are more than conquerors through him who loved us. For I am convinced that neither death, nor life, nor angels, nor rulers, nor things present, nor things to come, nor powers, nor height, nor depth, nor anything else in all creation, will be able to separate us from the love of God in Christ Jesus our Lord (Romans 8:31b-35, 37-39).

PRAYER FOR LIGHT

All good and gracious God,
we open ourselves
to the brilliance of your love.

Make our sin-darkened hearts white as snow.

As flame glows through crystal,
so let your light and goodness shine in us.

May you be praised and glorified
for ever and ever! Amen.